Wedding Tour

Emily and Dearman in Naples, 11 March 1873, photographed by Raffaello Ferretti. (see page 63)

Wedding Tour

January–June
1873
and
Visit to the Vienna Exhibition
Emily Birchall

Edited
by
David Verey

ALAN SUTTON · Gloucester
ST. MARTIN'S PRESS · New York

Copyright © 1985 Rosemary Verey

First published in Great Britain 1985
  Alan Sutton Publishing Limited
  30 Brunswick Road
  Gloucester GL1 1JJ

British Library Cataloguing in Publication Data

Birchall, Emily
  Wedding tour, January–June 1873.
  1. Europe—Description and travel—1800–1918
  I. Title   II. Verey, David
  914'.04287   D919

  ISBN 0-86299-208-7

First published in the United States of America 1985
  St. Martin's Press, Inc.
  175 Fifth Avenue
  New York, NY 10010

  ISBN 0-312-85998-8

Jacket picture: Custom House, Venice,
by J. Whitacre Allen

Typesetting and origination by
Alan Sutton Publishing Limited.
Printed in Great Britain.

Contents

Introduction

Emily was like a meteor, seen as a brilliant light by some people and then extinguished. She lived for the first thirty two years of the second half of the nineteenth century. Born on July 19th 1852, she died on September 2nd 1884. Born in clover, she married a rich man who was able to satisfy her enthusiasm for living, and her ardent quest for knowledge.

John Jowitt, her father, was a well-to-do Quaker merchant in Leeds and she was his fourth daughter. John was educated at a very good Quaker school at Tottenham. At the age of fifteen he went into the family business of wool-stapling, which had continued through five generations. He had by that time acquired a very fair knowledge of classics and, we are told, could read Homer and Horace with ease and pleasure, and the New Testament in Greek. His marriage to Deborah Benson in 1836 was one of unclouded happiness. Although an excellent man of business he found time to undertake innumerable works of charity which included such distressing tasks as visiting the sick-poor in Leeds for a Benevolent Society, and the year after his marriage he founded the Leeds Town Mission.

John and Deborah's family consisted of one son and three daughters. There then came a gap caused by the infant deaths of no less than five little boys before Emily and her younger sister Florence were born. In 1859 the family moved to Harehills Grove, a large Regency house standing in its own park though not far from the centre of the city. It is now known as Potternewton Mansion and the park is a public open space.

John Jowitt delighted in using his grounds for charitable purposes. When a thousand Sunday-school children assembled we are told 'he took joyfully the spoiling of his goods in the way of trampling down the shrubberies and grass, and the debris of orange-peel and bits of paper left behind.' Normally, however, the park was a private paradise for his children.

Nobody could ever have had a more affectionate parent than Emily's father. By the time Emily and Florence were growing up the three elder girls were married and John wrote regularly the most charming and loving letters to them. Often he would tell them what he was doing with his younger daughters.

On May 26th 1866 he wrote 'We have just returned from a long ride through Harewood and Eccup, splendid afternoon, wind most refreshing though the sun hot, trees in perfection and the ground covered with hyacinths. Oh darling we have such fun. Emily rides Fairy and Florence Bluebell as the former remarks it looks better as they are then nearer of a height. We had a lovely gallop on the green sward and down the lanes we saunter on lovingly, I in the middle, E hold of one arm and F of the other which causeth Emily to quote Milton declaring Papa is 'linked sweetness long drawn out', whereat Papa laughs immoderately and F. pronounces it "not bad." But I almost grudge this celestial weather without any of our wedded darlings here to enjoy it with us.'

John was a very fair artist and he made some delightful paintings for his children, of which 'Emily's farmyard' is an evocative survivor. As well as giving them great affection he and his wife provided a cultured and comfortable background for the children to grow up in, and an assured religious faith. They had governesses when they were young; but it is said John often had to teach the governess Latin as well as the children. Above everything, he inspired them with his own

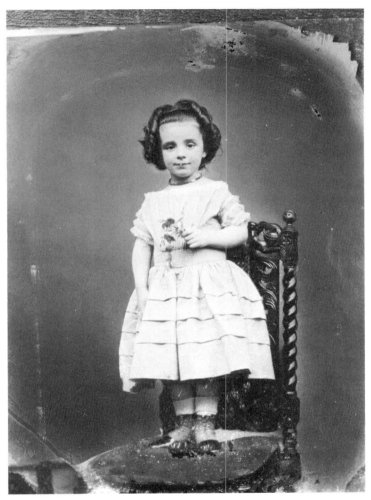

Emily as a child

Emily's farmyard by her father, John Jowitt

unquenchable religious beliefs. They were not kept at home all the time, and even the girls went to boarding schools.[1] Emily must have been away at school when her family visited her future husband's establishment.

On July 6th 1867 John wrote to a married daughter. 'The only event in our even tenor was visiting Dearman Birchall yesterday. We went early, Mamma, Florence and I with Benson and Carrie (son and daughter-in-law) as super-cargo. Dearman hailed us in Gipton Wood, riding up much as Robin Hood might have done, in 1400 and something, to the carriage door. But he soon put spurs to his black mare and we reached Scarcroft without any other encounters.

'After dinner we mounted the leads instead of sitting over the wine, and saw York Minster and the Yorkshire wolds beyond, and then had a regular inspection of the house from the boxroom to the pantry and saw no end of things from Paris, enough to fit up a travelling museum. Outside we went over the vineries and orchard houses, through the wood and across a perilous bridge between two streams – not to say rivers, at the confluence of which is an oval fishpond with an everplaying fountain in the middle and a ram at the other end to force up the water to Dearman's bathroom, a very admirable contrivance, much coveted for Harehills. A hasty tea and off home in the lovely twilight and moonlight.'

Dearman Birchall, a cloth-merchant, was John Jowitt's second cousin and they often met in Leeds; but Dearman was not yet particularly aware of Emily. She would then have been only fifteen. We do not know when she left school, or how she studied thereafter. She went abroad with her parents in 1870 for we hear of her in Mentone in April of that year. By the time she was twenty she had sat the Cambridge Examination for

---

[1] *The Diary of a Victorian Squire*, August 13 1874: Mr Justice Lush took Emily into dinner and was interested to hear she had been at Miss Taylor's school.

Women, in which she obtained first class honours, distinguished in divinity, literature, and French. Such success for a woman must have been unusual, and it had come to the attention of Matthew Arnold. Writing home on her honeymoon in Rome on April 14th 1873 she says, 'I reintroduced myself to Mr. Arnold and he remembered me at once and was most pleasant and talked about my exams which he seemed to know all about. But I hear you are no longer Miss Jowitt, he said, so I introduced Dearman.'

The manner in which Dearman and Emily became engaged is described by Dearman in his diary which was published under the title *The Diary of a Victorian Squire* in 1983. On October 8th 1872 Dearman attended a Church Congress in Leeds. He had become a member of the Church of England, having left the Quakers, at the time of his first marriage in 1861. Most of John Jowitt's family had also joined the church. On October 7th he had dined at John Jowitt's – no mention of Emily. However, on October 11th he writes, 'Conversazione held this evening. On going into the Victoria Hall I found it very crowded. One of the first persons I encountered was Emily Jowitt alone. Following the impulse of the moment I offered her my arm and we spent the evening walking about together. She was very sociable and pleasant and I was much smitten with her. Though very short-sighted her eyes were bright and luminous and worked on my imagination after I had parted from her with regret.'

Two days later Dearman and his architect brother Edward went to Harehills and picked up Emily and Florence taking them to Chapeltown Church. Emily looked bewitching in church and Dearman screwed himself round in their box-pew so he was better able to stare at her. On their way home Florence and Edward made themselves scarce and Emily became communicative complaining presumably that she did not see where her academic success was leading her. 'Oh that she was a man and had a career.' 'The impulse of Friday night still possessed me,' writes Dearman, 'and wandering up and down the Harehills gardens I asked her to accept the mission of living with me.' There was no immediate reply.

At first the Jowitts demurred because of the disparity of their ages; Dearman was forty four and Emily only twenty. Emily's mother Deborah, however, was soon saying she had always preferred middle-aged men to young ones. They were fond of Dearman anyway, and he was a good match, having recently bought a beautiful estate in Gloucestershire and retired from full-time participation in his Leeds business. It was also sad that he had been a widower for so long, with one motherless daughter. The way became clear, and they were married early in the new year, January 1873; but not before both Dearman and Emily had had private soul-searchings, and had become convinced of the depth of each other's character.

The scene was now set for the six month honeymoon tour. Emily was probably so well versed in composing essays that writing presented no problems, for she wrote long letters as well as the journal throughout the period, and she did not repeat herself. In addition to her thorough knowledge of French, she was credited with knowing five other languages, and Dearman very soon called her the Polyglot. The English people they met were often acquaintances they made at the *table d'hôte* of the hotels they stayed in. Mr. M.M. Warburg was one of Dearman's business partners. He had had him to stay in Gloucestershire in the May of the previous year. His function seems to have been that of a travelling salesman and so their rendezvous with him was obviously previously arranged. Dearman, at that time, thought he did a good job. The young Oswald Birchall was also in favour. He was the twenty-three year old son of Dearman's first cousin Edwin, to please whom he had been taken in to the business as a junior partner. He was sent to Vienna to prepare the exhibition; but by the time the Birchalls arrived he had been able to do nothing owing to the non-appearance of the stands sent from England. When they did eventually arrive Dearman was disappointed. 'The sameness of our patterns strikes me and I feel most disappointed that not a single thing has been made for it or anything done but sending a nice assortment of the plain everyday things we are usually selling.' A little bit of business was combined with much pleasure, and the pattern was set for the rest of their married life. Fortunately, neither of them could see it would hardly last twelve years, and Emily very soon discovered she had the most delightful companion possible, while he never ceased to be surprised and dazzled by her.

CHAPTER I

Paris, the South of France
Northern Italy

Dearman Birchall and Emily Jowitt were married on January 22nd 1873 at the parish church in Leeds and spent the first few days thereafter at Brown's Hotel in London.

Saturday, 25 January.   We left Charing Cross station at 1.25, having there met our courier, but too late for him to register the luggage, so that we were obliged to take it on just as it was, trusting to have time to register it at Boulogne.

We had a remarkably pleasant crossing, the day being bright and fine, but the air grew very cold as we neared the end of the passage. We had not left Folkestone till 4.50, owing to some delay, as we ought to have started at 3.55. There was therefore so little time at Boulogne before the 6.55 train to Paris that though we managed to get some dinner Perrini could not register the luggage in time, so remained behind with it, whilst we came on to Paris, with nothing but our *sacs de nuit.* We reached the Grand Hotel about midnight. On the boat, we had been much struck by the number of French gentlemen, evidently returning from the Emperor's funeral.[2] Among them was one splendid old general, remarkably like the late

---

[2] Napoleon III died at Chislehurst on 9th January.

Emperor in face, who never moved a single feature, but wore a constant expression of sadness and fortitude.

Sunday, 26 January.   After breakfast in the cafe, we went to church in the Rue d'Agnesseau, and were surprized to find there a very large congregation. Coming out of church, we fell in with Mr. and Mrs. Underwood (we had met Mr. Underwood on the boat) and they were most cordial and friendly. They asked us to dinner, but we compromised the matter by arranging to lunch with them next day. On parting from them we took a delightful walk along the Rue Royale and the Rue St Honoré, through the Champs Elysees, down past the vacant place where stood the Ministère de la Finance, then past the Tuileries, where we stood still to gaze on what seemed to me the most harrowing sight I had ever seen, that noble building with all its historic associations, now ruined, roofless, charred and desolate, with here and there a scrap of marble chimney piece, or a bit of wall-paper, or a broken pane of glass, appearing among the ruins.[3] The Louvre is almost untouched. We then made our way through the Palais Royal (the palace there also in ruins) by the Rue Richelieu, along the Boulevard, past the Madeleine, back to church, to the 3.30 service, after which we called on the Grahams at the Hotel de Ville St d'Albion, but unfortunately found them not at home and then returned to our hotel.

Two things struck us very much that afternoon, the one being the fact that the great majority of the shops were closed, which made the streets seem much quieter than on Sundays of yore, the other, the apparently real reverence, and melancholy interest, with which the crowds gathered round the portraits of "L'Empereur Napoleon III" in all the photograph shops, and gazed on the dead face of their mighty master.

---

[3] The war with Prussia began in July 1870 and Napoleon III surrendered in September.

We dined at the *Table d'hôte*, in the beautiful *Salle à manger*, about 250 were there, of whom the vast majority were French; English and Americans being few and far between. We had a quiet evening, with a bright fire in our charming room *au premier*.

Monday, 27 January. We left by train for St. Cloud at 11.30, meeting Mr. Underwood at the St. Lazare station. On our arrival at their pretty little house (which had been utterly destroyed in the war) we had a most *recherché* luncheon, served in the most perfect style, and then they accompanied us through the town, where the desolation exceeds anything I had ever imagined, reminding one of Pompei in its complete-ness. Whole streets reduced to heaps of stones, though all who saw it two years ago say that the appearance of it now is wonderfully different, as they are working hard at rebuilding it. We then went to the Castle, which is in a deplorable state of ruin and desolation. Nothing has yet been done to rebuild it, and the broken lamps, battered balconies, scraps of splendid marble chimney-pieces, &c &c. remain just as they were left in 1870.

From St. Cloud we drove round by Auteuil to the Porte Maillot and then past the Arc de Triomphe down the Champs Elysees back to our hotel. That evening we went to the Opera, and saw *La coupe de Roi de Thule* which we enjoyed immensely, the singing was good, especially Faures', and the scenery perfectly lovely. The scene, the dome of the Sirens *au fond de la mer* was exquisite in the highest degree. We had capital places, though the house was crowded. We walked home, and found lots of letters awaiting us at the hotel.

Tuesday, 28 January. We walked about for some time, down the Boulevard Sebastopol, calling on Mr. Priestley, and then to the café Voisin, where Mr. Warburg[4] met us. We had asked

---

[4] Dearman's business partner.

him to dinner, but as he was engaged for every evening (once to meet M. Thiers[5] at a party) we invited him to lunch with us, and we found him extremely pleasant and amusing. After a long lengthy luncheon we went to see the ruins of the Hotel de Ville, and then walked slowly back to our hotel. A great many more English than heretofore, appeared at the *Table d'hôte*. We had a quiet evening, writing letters &c. The day was very bright and sunny and fine, but exceedingly cold, though there was no frost.

Wednesday, 29 January.   We drove to Sèvres – starting before 11, after receiving a call from Mr. Warburg, to see the modern china there, and the still more interesting museum, which contains a splendid collection of oriental, (some Persian plates over which Dearman raved) Spanish, Palissy, a little Henri II, Maiolica, &c. &c.

After spending several hours most pleasantly here, we drove back to Paris, stopping in the Champs Elysees to see the most marvellous Panorama I ever beheld. It was a view of the siege of Paris, and we were supposed to be standing on Fort Issy, the fort being at the time under Prussian fire. Immediately around us were the earth works of the fort, all busy with life and action, groups of soldiers strengthening the *fascines,* others reconnoitring through loop holes, others firing the cannon, and one party carrying away the body of a young officer who had just been killed by a shell bursting within the fort. Then outside the lines lay the deserted country, abandoned villages, some standing in ruins, and others smouldering, others actually in flames, giving one a vivid realization of the horrors of war. Then beyond this stretch of country lay, on one side, the city of Paris, with the Invalides, the Arc de Triomphe, the

---

[5] Louis-Adolphe Thiers (1796–1877), statesman, journalist, and historian, first President of the third Republic, 1871–3.

Panthéon, Notre-Dame, &c. &c. Behind it the heights of Montmartre and Belleville, and, all round the horizon the forts of Bicêtre, Montrouge, Montretout, and Mount Velérien, some quite silent, others sending forth dense clouds of smoke from their cannon. Altogether it was the most wonderful thing I ever saw in my life, and so extraordinarily well painted that it was impossible not to fancy that one was looking on actual reality. I don't remember ever being so impressed by anything; with my strong feelings on the subject, it was deeply interesting to see it all laid before our eyes.

That evening we left the Grand Hotel immediately after dining at the *Table d'hôte,* and started from the Lyons station, at 8 p.m. We had a *coupé lit* to ourselves, and were most comfortable, both of us sleeping as well as possible from 10.30 till 6.30, with the exception of a break at Dijon at 1.30 to refresh our inner men with some *café au lait.* We have agreed that we both exceedingly enjoy travelling by night.

Thursday, 30 January. We breakfasted at Lyons at 7 a.m. and then travelled on; but it was difficult to believe we were going southwards, for we saw snow on the hills and then on the ground at Valence, the first we had seen since we left Leeds. It was intensely cold all the way, so that we were glad of all our wraps, and when we reached Marseilles, it was raining pretty heavily, so that my impressions on re-entering the city were very different from those with which I had quitted it in 1870.

We found very nice rooms engaged for us at the Grand Hotel de Marseilles, and after dining with only about a dozen others (chiefly Americans of the worst class), we spent a quiet evening in our own room.

Friday, 31 January. After breakfast we had a delicious drive up the Prado and round past the Château d'If to the Port, and then visited and were much disappointed with the Zoological

Gardens. We wandered about the ill-kept paths, in vain searched after creatures in general, and Mark Twain's celebrated stork[6] in particular, but the only animals we could find were some dilapidated pheasants, two emaciated giraffes, a dirty sheep, a few canaries, a seedy bantam, and a dyspeptic looking Black Spanish cock.

We soon returned to the Hotel in disgust.

Leaving Marseilles at 1.15, we did not reach Cannes till 7.15, though Toulon, Hyères and Fréjus are the only intermediate places of the slightest interest. We did full justice to our 8.50 dinner.

Saturday, 1 February.   We have most comfortable quarters at the Grand Hotel de Cannes, which I think far superior to the Beau Site, though I prefer the West to the East side.

We met at breakfast Mr. R. Green and his cousin Mr. Chas. Green, their respective spouses being ill in bed. We knew Mr. & Mrs. R. Green were here, and we have found them and their cousins most kind and pleasant. Mr. R. Green accompanied us to the Villa S. George, where we had some difficulty in getting in, as dear old M. Granvalle is dead, but at last we sent in our cards, with a humble request for special permission, and were graciously admitted. The garden is as lovely as ever, roses, camellias, and primulas blooming in the greatest luxuriance in the bright Southern sunshine, and the deep blue sea before us in all its brilliant beauty. The day was absolutely perfect, very hot, but with a delicious breeze, and we all expended an immense amount of pity on the unfortunates who are shivering in England whilst

---

[6] *Innocents Abroad* (1870) chapter XI, pages 72–3: 'A sort of tall, long-legged bird with a beak like a powder-horn, and close-fitting wings like the tails of a dress coat. This fellow stood up with his eyes shut and his shoulders stooped forward a little, and looked as if he had his hands under coat tails.

we are luxuriating in this glorious climate. By and by Mr. Green left us, and we went up to the Croix de la Garde – my dear old favourite walk and had the superb view as lovely as ever from the top. We were back to lunch at two, and then at three Mr. R. Green and Mrs. C. Green accompanied us in a delightful walk towards Antibes, to the Villa Scott, from the tower of which we had a most glorious viw of Antibes, Villa Franca (Villefranche), and the Maritime Alps on the East, with Cannes and the lovely Esterels on the West. We were not home till 5.30

At 6 o'clock *Table d'hôte* we sat with the four Greens at the head of the table, and afterwards we spent a very pleasant evening with them in their salon, and were a most lively party, having coffee, ices, music, and much conversation. They are here for the health of Mrs. R. Greeen and Mr. Charles Green, a clergyman with one of the most beautiful faces I ever saw. I am as charmed with Cannes as ever.

Sunday, 2 February. In the morning, after meeting the Greens at breakfast, Dearman and I went to Mr. Rolfe's church, a long way from this hotel. The service was delightful, the singing lovely, and Mr. Rolfe gave us a very nice short sermon. The church was crowded, and we sat on chairs in the aisle. The heat was something tremendous. A collection was made for the Marseilles Sailors' Home, and nearly £50 was taken in the morning.

After lunch we went again to the same church, and heard a stranger preach; there was a good congregation, though of course not so large nearly as that of the morning. After church we called on the Greens, and had a very pleasant chat with them, renewed at dinner. We spent the evening quietly reading and writing in our own room. The visitors here seem very nice, pleasant and sociable; chiefly English, some French and a very few Americans. Another bride and bridegroom,

Lord and Lady Jersey,[7] are here, and there are swarms of couriers in the house.

Monday, 3 February. After breakfast we said goodbye to Mrs. C. Green, and the two gentlemen accompanied us to the station, whence we departed at 11.30 for Nice. In our carriage were five English gentlemen, all going to the races at Nice. They were extremely pleasant, especially one, a good deal like Major Bonnor. We crossed over at a snail's pace the temporary bridge over the river into which that unfortunate train plunged just a year ago, when the bridge had been washed away by the torrent. Even now traces of the terrible accident are strewn all around and they seem extremely dilatory about rebuilding the bridge.

We reached Nice before one, and drove at once to the *Poste Restante,* (Perrini conveying the luggage to the Hotel meanwhile) where we found 17 most welcome letters, which, after a week's complete dearth, were highly acceptable. They were from Papa, Mama, Benson, Carrie, Dora and Susie, Florrie, Aunt E.M., Mrs. Brook, Edward, Coz. Eliza, Helen, Allie, &c. and we greatly enjoyed reading them all.

After lunch at the Hotel de Rome, where we have a nice room with full view of the glorious sea, we went to the Villa Bardin, to call on Maida's[8] relatives, called Muir, and found them all at home. Their house is beautifully situated above the town. Then we walked and drove about a little, till it was time for dinner. This was rather a mild affair, very poor menu, and company small and uninteresting. In the evening we virtuously set to work, both of us, and wrote letters as hard as we could go, and so absorbing was our occupation, that we were

---

[7] Victor, 7th Earl of Jersey married Margaret, daughter of Lord Leigh of Stoneleigh, September 19th 1872.

[8] Maida Mirrielees was an intimate school-friend of Emily's.

blissfully unconscious of the flight of time, so that when at last, all our labours done, we had leisure to think of sublunary concerns, and bethought ourselves of claiming the reward of the just in the shape of tea and coffee respectively, we rang the bell, to find it answered by a sleepy-looking youth who stared aghast at our request, and it was only after he had disappeared mysteriously into the kitchen regions that we made the startling discovery that it was long after 11 p.m., so we were not surprised to hear on his return that it was *trop tard* and resigned ourselves philosophically to go thirsting to bed. He must have thought us highly eccentric.

Tuesday, 4 February.   This has been one of the red letter days of my life, having been signalized by a glorious walk, in magnificent scenery, on an absolutely perfect day, and with a most congenial companion. What more could be desired? After a long discussion on ways and means yesterday with Perrini, we suddenly started the brilliant idea that we would *walk* to Mentone, whilst he and the luggage came by train. Our faithful Italian threw up his hands and eyes, gasped for breath, and all but fainted on the spot. At last, after having vainly tried to dissuade us from so suicidal an enterprize, he resigned us to our fate, washing his hands of us, and evidently regarding us as a couple of amiable lunatics.

So this morning we started directly after breakfast, i.e. at 11 a.m. by Nice time ($\frac{1}{2}$ an hour later than ours) and had a most exhilarating and delightful walk, intensely enjoyed by both of us. The steep first part of the ascent was the only place where we really found the sun excessively hot. There I mounted parasol and veil, and doffed gloves and all doffable garments, and Dearman peeled to his shirt sleeves, greatly exciting my envy of his cool and airy appearance. The heat was however by no means oppressive, as there was all the time a most delicious breeze. The views the whole way were of course perfectly enchanting, and delighted me even more than they did three years ago, for one sees them so much more satisfactorily when on foot than from a carriage. As we mounted the Turbia, the long stretch of blue sea, with all its charming bays and capes, Villa-franca below us to our right, beyond that Nice, then the Cap d'Antibes running far out to sea, beyond again the islands opposite Cannes, further still the exquisite Esterels with their grand outlines, and farthest of all the hills just on this side of Marseilles, while looking inland, our eyes feasted on the lovely snowy peaks of the Maritime Alps, and, nearer, on the olive covered hills, the terraced vineyards and the scattered cottages of the country round Nice, – all this made up a superb picture, seen as it was on a day of such brilliance.

We reached the excessively picturesque village of Turbia [Turbie] soon after 2.30, and remained there nearly an hour, baiting ourselves. We ventured to enter an awfully seedy looking restaurant, where we found an untidy but amiable landlady who covered the little wooden table with a clean white tablecloth, and gave us knives and plated forks and even dinner-napkins, and, by and by, very good hard-boiled eggs, bread and nice sweet *vin du pays* which last exactly suited my taste, and to all of which fare we did full justice.

The descent to Mentone exhausted us just as much as the ascent from Nice, the view of sea and land, of Monaco far down to our right, Roccabruna [Roquebrune] the romantic, down in front, Mentone further on, and the lovely coastline ending with bright sunny Bordighera, and of the grand soft grey and warm yellow of the fine heights above us standing out against the dark-blue sky, being perfectly ravishing.

The day had been so summer-like that we were positively surprized when we became suddenly conscious that the sun was setting, reminding us that we are still in the first season of the year. The latter part of the walk was made in the darkening twilight, for we did not reach Mentone till nearly six. We were received by Perrini, who was anxiously looking out for us, having evidently expected either to hear of our demise, or to see us brought in on litters, in a state of collapse. We have taken up our quarters at the Hotel Victoria.

Wednesday, 5 February.   A most charming day. We strolled about Mentone for some time after breakfast, marvelling at the amount of damage done by the recent storms, that strong sea-wall in the East bay washed away by the waves, the promenade in part destroyed &c. We then climbed the hill, up those narrow stair-streets to the cemetery, whence we had a glorious view; there is much more snow on the hills than when we were here before. At 12.40 we took the train for Monaco, after more than half an hour's wait at the station, for we had gone by Mentone time, forgetting that the trains went by Paris. We shall be thankful to get into Italy, when we may have some chance of being able to ascertain what time it is.

At present we are in a hopeless state, since every clock we see tells a different tale; at the Nice station there were in all *five* clocks, no two of them within 10 minutes of one another. We did not stop at Monte Carlo, but went on to Monaco, and there took a pretty little basket with a pair of frisky ponies, and drove round the miniature sovereignty, through the lovely gardens, and then to the Casino.

Monte Carlo was unusually gay, owing to a pigeon shooting match that was going on there so we saw it under its most gorgeous aspect, crowded with the fast and fashionable, the ladies in toilettes of the most magnificent description conceivable, and all under the cloudless bright blue sky.

We watched the pigeon-shooting for a little while, but thought it very poor sport. The birds were shut up, one at a time, in little traps, about 20 yards from the sportsmen, and on a string being pulled, the trap opened, and the pigeon flew out, to be immediately brought down, for it hardly ever rose a yard into the air before it was hit, though one or two birds managed to get clear away untouched. We soon had seen as much of this as we wished, and repaired to the Casino, there to become very soon absorbed in the intense interest either of watching the different faces round the tables, or else of following the fortunes of some one man. We found those who played highest the most attractive, and there certainly was a great deal of high play going on. We watched one very handsome young man for a long time; he won at first, very largely indeed, and had no end of notes, rouleaux and napoleons before him, but then the luck turned, and he lost each coup, every time turning paler, and biting his lips, till at last *all* was gone, he had not a single napoleon left, and then he rose and walked away. Another quite old man, English, played desperately and apparently without any system or plan, and we saw him do nothing but lose, note after note, always 1000 francs at least; he seemed to be terribly unlucky, but we were told he had won far more than he had lost. We stood for $1\frac{1}{2}$ hours watching an English gentleman at rouge et noir, with the deepest interest. He played evidently on a regular system, entering everything in a book, and very high too, for we several times saw him stake as much as £200 at once. He won 20,000 francs whilst we watched him.

We dined at the *Table d'hôte* in the handsome dining hall; about 300 there, and a very good dinner.

Afterwards we watched the play again, and then left at 9.50, or ought to have done, but the train was half an hour late, so we had another long wait at the station. We hear that the tables made £9,000 sterling one day last week. The whole affair is kept up in the most luxurious style, reading rooms, concert rooms, &c.; but it certainly must pay the Prince very well.

Thursday, 6 February.   Left Mentone at 10.30, and drove to San Remo, where we arrived about two. The road was in one or two places very bad, from avalanches of earth having fallen on it. We 'put up' at the Hotel Victoria, and found it fairly comfortable, though I did not care for the people – so far as one could judge – so much as the Hôtel de Londres set three years ago. After lunch we went to Villa Speranza, and had a very pleasant call on the Wedderburns. Lady Wedderburn[9] is a charming old lady, and the daughters very nice. We had afternoon tea there, and they were most friendly and agreeable. Then we went to call on C.E. Baines, and had a very pleasant chat with her and Mrs. Daubeny. She was very warm and nice, and looks pretty well, decidedly better than when in England.

After making these calls, we went down to the end of the Mola, and saw the magnificent sunset very well. I don't think I ever saw the sky more brilliant, and the reflections on the sea, and the red glow on the Eastern hills, were most lovely. At the *Table d'hôte* a lady bowed to Dearman, and he returned the salute, but without having the vaguest idea who she was, though to both of us her face seemed familiar. There was a young lady there talking so animatedly to a young man, that we immediately fixed on them as a certain newly married couple for whom C.E. Baines had told us to look out, and we watched them a good deal, and felt proudly thankful that we were not given to betray ourselves by such open spooning in public.

After dinner the youth came up to Dearman, and announced himself as the son of Mr. W.E. Swaine of Leeds, and it turned out that the lady who had bowed was his sister, and the 'bride' merely a lady they had met in the hotel. He was much amused and evidently flattered, to find what impression he and his neighbour had made on us. We feel pretty sure it is a 'case'.

---

[9] A Gloucestershire friend of Dearman's.

Next morning Dearman had a long chat with the Swaines, and their cousin Miss Paget, in their salon, and he took me in to see them. They were all most pleasant. Altogether we have had a good deal of sociability here.

Friday, 7 February.   We left San Remo at 11.45 and did not reach Genoa (by train all the way) till 6.15. The extreme slowness of this journey is partly owing to the dangerous state of the line, which in some places obliges the trains to go very carefully. We crept through one long tunnel in pitch darkness, as, of course, our lamp had gone out (as many lamps have, in a tunnelly journey, by the by) and were cheered beforehand by the comforting remark from the guard that the tunnel *might fall in* – it did so last week. However, on this occasion it didn't, and just beyond it the train had to be divided, and taken in two pieces over a very unsafe piece of line, and at another point the rail was propped up with *sandbags,* in military fashion, and we saw many places where landslips had carried away the lines, or the rains washed away the embankments, these breakages being only temporarily repaired. We stopped an infinite number of times, for it seems to be the rule to pull up and have five or ten minutes *d'attente* at every little village. The very last part of the journey was especially tedious, as we stopped between Voltri and Genoa no less than five times. We took up our quarters on our arrival, at the Hôtel d'Italie, which we find so extremely comfortable that we cannot think of leaving tomorrow for Pisa, as we had intended, and therefore decided to spend Sunday here.

Saturday, 8 February. Perrini is a source of perpetual amusement to us, he indulges in considerable exaggerations, and the strongest expressions, but always with the same genial face, and he never loses his temper in the slightest degree. He frequently uses the threat 'if he doesn't do it, I will break his neck' and profusely bestows such mild epithets as vagabond, rascal, scoundrel, &c &c. Whilst we were in France, he found a reason for every ill that befell us, in the fact that the country enjoyed the Republican form of government; if a hotel-keeper made an exorbitant charge, he was a republican, if the candles would not light, they were revolutionary, if the coffee was smoked, a republican had prepared it. We thought his spirits would rise on crossing the Pont St. Louis frontier, and entering a Kingdom, but no, Italy is no better, 'Sir, we are in Italy' is thought sufficient explanation for any misadventure, 'a nation of liars' he calmly calls his own compatriots, for he is a Genoaese by birth. He *considers* himself English, however, and such is the strength of his devotion that he 'would rather be dead in England than alive in any other country.' So much so, that he has invested his little all in the purchase of 'some land in England – a small freehold, – at Brompton, – I pay no taxes for it, – it is *in the cemetery,* Sir'! He said this afternoon, 'This is a charming country, so enlightened, so intelligent, I daresay I might find in it somewhere a *newspaper of last year'.* He was able to console himself for the horror of our walking to Mentone the other day only by the reflection that 'these English, they have legs of steel', and when I remarked 'it is not so very far; it is a good walk', 'Yes, Madame, you are perfectly right, it *is* a good walk, a *very* good walk. I call it not walking; I call it killing'. When he heard that Dearman had taken off his coat for the walk, he nearly expired. 'Thank you Sir, I am very much obliged to you – Oh! yes, an excellent thing, Sir, an admirable thing, if you want to get an inflamation.' His accent, and manner of speaking, are irresistibly comic, and he amuses us endlessly.

We have today our first quiet day; it rained all the morning, for a wonder, so we sat in our nice cosy room and diligently wrote letters, and then this afternoon when it cleared up and we were thinking of going out, we discovered that the *table d'hôte* was at the unearthly hour of five, so there was not time. There are apparently very few people staying at this house, the only ones at the *table d'hôte* besides ourselves were an American bishop, an English canon and his wife, a young married English couple, three French people, and a very pleasant English gentleman next me. There are others in the house, however, for we see them about. This is a most comfortable, and remarkably well conducted hotel.

Sunday, 9 February. I am in constant fear of repeating in my journal the sad history of that of the immortal Jack, in the *Innocents Abroad.* [10] Dearman holds its melancholy fate in terror over me, and seeing that I am now a whole week behind (I write in Rome, on the 15th) my journal is beginning to weigh like a nightmare on my mind. I must at once whet my scythe, and begin to mow down the accumulated week's growth in double quick time.

We went to morning and afternoon service in the pretty little new English church, of which Dearman's old friend Mr. Strettell is Chaplain, and the service was very nicely conducted. We spoke to Mr. & Mrs. Strettell, and they were very pleasant, pressing us to stay another day and dine with them on Monday, &c. &c. Between the services, and after evening prayer, we did a good deal of walking about in the gardens, on the promenade, and in the town, visiting a good many of the churches, and 'such-like' till it was almost dinner-time. In the evening we had a pleasant call from Mr. Strettell. We met at dinner and at church the Bishop of Ohio, whose acquaintance we had made on arriving at Genoa. On this day we learned more of our faithful Perrini's history than

---

[10] Mark Twain (1870) chapter IV, page 256. Jack began a voluminous journal but abandoned it when he reckoned he was as much as four thousand pages behind hand!

we had known before. He has had three wives, the first an Italian, who ran away with a priest (thence his bitter hatred against the order) the second a Swiss, who died 10 weeks after the marriage, the present one English, who has a baby.

Monday, 10 February.   We left Genoa by 10 a.m. train, and had a most glorious journey through that very fine part of the Riviera di Levante, as far as Sestri, where the railway comes to an end. There we made an attempt at luncheon, and our spirits rose to see a long table set out as for a *table d'hôte* and with napkins, knives and forks, &c. certainly all a trifle dingy, but serving to promise something eatable. Our hearts soon died within us, however, on the apparition of *du rosbif* (as some nasty grey little bits of dog were by courtesy termed) and some very greasy potatoes, with sour wine, bread of the consistency of leather, and of a very singular flavour, and butter made of lard, garlic, and oil, I should think.

Having regaled ourselves as best we could on these luscious *viands, nous nous mènes en voyage,* the last but one to depart of the five carriage-loads for Spezzia, and we soon became the last, for we had only three horses and were passed by a great travelling carriage with five or six. The road was very heavy, in consequence of the melting of the deep snow which had recently covered it, so that our progress was much slower than we had anticipated. Dearman walked a good part of the way, as it is nearly all up hill, and we only went at a foot's pace. It was an exquisite day, and we enjoyed the drive excessively, but unfortunately night fell before we reached the finest part, so that we saw a mere moonlight shadow of that glorious view just above Spezzia. The moon was most brilliant, and it was as delightful an evening as we could possibly have had. It seemed a perfect farce for our driver to stop and light his lamps, just before we entered Spezzia, but he told us that no carriages were allowed to drive in the town without them. The night air was so cold that we were glad of all our wraps, and not less glad on arriving at the Hôtel de Milan, of a good warm fire, for that touchingly considerate Perrini, having observed that Madame had a cold, had telegraphed for a fire to be ready for us. We did not reach Spezzia till just before nine, perfectly ravenous, and thankful to find a first rate dinner all ready. We had left Sestri at 1 p.m.

Tuesday, 11 February. At a quarter to five there comes a knock at our door, blending itself with my peaceful dreams, but answered at once by the wakeful Dearman, who had been up and dressing I know not how long, and who on opening the door, beholds Perrini, fully dressed, not even the inevitable cloak omitted, and informing us that we must be ready at 5.45. On his departure, Dearman imparts this sad news to me, who receive it sulkily and sleepily, but murmur my intention of arising on the instant. I then try to go to sleep again, but am frustrated by my vigilant spouse, who persists in talking to me, and urging me to get up. I then resign myself to my fate, and groan for 20 minutes, doubtless to the great edification of an Englishman in the next room, whom I hear splashing in his bath, and whistling cheerily. How I *hate* that heartless whistling! At last, having groaned till I am tired, without producing any impression on my husband's heart of adamant, I tumble out of bed, and pity myself profusely all the while I am dressing until I suddenly become aware that I am fearfully late, by Perrini's coming for the luggage before I have begun my hair. I finish my toilette with the greatest precipitancy, lock my box, which is instantly carried off to the omnibus, and then I descend to take what breakfast I can at that unearthly hour, and we drive off to the station in the moonlight.

Our train starts at six, we are in plenty of time and find a carriage secured for us by the ever ready Perrini. By this time I find myself particularly wakeful and lively, and look out anxiously for the sunrise, which however we do not see very well, as the orb of the day rises just in front of our engine. Why we are at this moment going due east, passes our comprehension.

Pisa, 9.a.m. Here we changed carriages and finding we had an hour to wait, we drove off to see the dear old Cathedral and gaze once more upon that unrivalled trio of noble buildings Duomo, Baptistry and Campanile. We had no time to ascend the Leaning Tower, as I did with Aunt E.M.[11] three years ago. At Leghorn, where we arrived at 10.30, we expected to have another hour, so immediately took a carriage and started off to see the city, but our intentions were nipped in the bud, for we had scarcely gone 20 yards, when a porter rushed after us, and volubly adjured us to turn back, the courier said so because the train left at 11 o'clock. I, supposing him to be a gay deceiver (I had been told that all Italians are liars) treated this information with contempt, snubbed the porter, and declined to turn back. But our coachman, being more submissive to orders, turned, and drove us ignominiously back to the station, where Perrini met us, to confirm the story of the despised porter, whom he had himself sent to call us back! My shame and confusion of face, as I humbly descended from the carriage, and met the eyes of the grinning porter, can better be imagined than described. I felt small, the porter triumphed.

We had some pretty decent lunch at Leghorn (judging from the frequent mention of victuals and drink in this journal, our principal occupation would seem to be *meals*, rather prosaic for a wedding tour, when honey and nectar are supposed to be the only fitting viands for the poetic pair; we are *not* poetic, alas!) and started onwards at 11. In about an hour, we came to a place called Aquabuona, where every human being in the

[11] Esther-Maria Jowitt, John Jowitt's sister, who accompanied them on their tour in 1870.

crowded train had to turn out, and take to an omnibus, as the line was destroyed for about 4 kilometres, *last October,* by the inundations, and it will not be passable for 3 months more! It is a scene of wreck and ruin the whole way, and I should think three years more likely than three months, at the Italian rate of working, for they have not *begun* to repair it yet. After we had taken our places in the train that met us, we found we had still to wait more than half an hour, as the numerous omnibuses had to go back to bring the 3rd class passengers and the luggage. It was amusing to watch the crowd of porters carrying the luggage from the omnibus to the van. Of course one man could not possibly carry more than one article, so that each box, were it but a hat-box, engrossed the undivided attention of one man, 'they fear to overheat themselves; if they worked harder they might catch an inflammation', says Perrini in explanation. At last we were off again, our carriage full of people of the most deeply uninteresting description, ourselves of course excepted.

At Orbetello, at 5.30, we made a dash as did everybody else, at the Refreshment Room, in our usual pursuit of food, and such a *rush* I never saw; the waiters seemed 'fair maddled', and flew aimlessly about in the vain endeavour to answer some of the thousand calls upon them. I am sure half the people came away without paying in the end. Dearman might easily have done so, for finding himself absolutely destitute of funds, he rushed out, napkin in hand, and unpursued, to find Perrini who as usual was mounting guard on our luggage.

We were due at Rome about 9.40 p.m. but the train was a little late. It was an exquisite night, bright moonlight, all my companions slumbered and slept, and I sat looking out of the window, thinking of the old Latin races that once dwelt on these plains, of all the Etruscan armies that marched across them against Rome, and then of glorious Rome itself, as we crossed the yellow Tiber, and neared the Eternal city. It was a positive relief to me when we entered the busy modern station, and found it just like any other station; the feeling of being in Rome was so exciting that it was only the comfortable modernness of the petroleum lighted station, that prevented it from being overpowering. We drove through the moonlight streets to the Albergo di Russie.

CHAPTER II

Rome

Wednesday, 12 February. In Rome! the first thought when we awoke this morning, as it was the last when we closed our eyes at night. It seems almost too good to be true that the longing dreams of one's whole life should actually be realized. And the morning is so fresh and bright and sunny that Rome appears to us first under the most charming circumstances possible. It is far far more delightful in every way than we either of us expected, high as were our anticipations. It is such a bright, healthy feeling, *cheerful* city, such a *clean* place, so orderly, that even had it no historic associations, no monuments of art or antiquity whatever, it would still be, I think, the very pleasantest, charmingest spot on the face of the earth.

Rome is full – crowded. The landlord at the Russie has contrived to find us one room on the *entresal* for two days, but it is engaged for Friday, and he has no other hole or corner to offer us. We must turn out. Perrini goes round to all the best hotels, and hears everywhere the same tale. Full, full everywhere. Or perchance some tiny dingy back-room is shewn him, but we are not ambitious for such a lodging till we find we can get no better in the length and breadth of Rome. At last, by good luck, a suite is found, in one of the *dépendances* of the Hotel di Londra, of which we have heard that it is very good, but very expensive. We go to see the rooms, and thankfully engage them for tomorrow; they consist of a good sitting-room, bedroom and two dressing-rooms, on the ground floor, and looking on to the Piazza di Spagna. For today we remain at the Russie. The first place we go to is of course S. Peter's. Who could be twelve hours in Rome and keep away from her Cathedral? We walked to it, guided by Perrini (and pounced upon in the Corso by Dearman's widow-friend, Mrs. Hartley) over the Ponte di S. Angelo whence the first glimpse of the Dome came to us, and far from feeling the least touch of that disappointment which, so many say, accompanies the first sight of it, it filled me with wondering admiration. It was grander, huger, vaster than my dreams of it. We walked on till we stood in the glorious Piazza, with S. Peter's in front of us, its splendid colonnade on either side, and the Vatican to our right. We went into the Cathedral, and we stood still in sight of its vastness, breathless with awe and wonder. Dearman says he never felt so excited by anything in his life, and my feelings were certainly beyond description. The glorious majesty of the whole impresses one more than anything else, but besides this there is the individual beauty of every inch of roof and wall, pillar and floor, the exquisite taste of the decoration, the richness of the marbles, the loveliness of the frescoes, and the great beauty of the sculpture. The vastness of the scale of S. Peter's can only be appreciated when one sees in the distance at the other end of the nave, how tiny men and women look, and how small those statues or other objects, which one knows to be really of great size, appear at that distance. We were disgusted with the irreverence of one vulgar English tourist, who had seated himself, Murray in hand, on the top step of the High Altar itself, and just in front of the very altar.

On this first visit we did not attempt to see S. Peter's properly, but contented ourselves with the general impression of the whole. After lunch at the Russie Dearman went out for a stroll, and I spent the afternoon answering some of my letters, for I found a famous budget awaiting me, some addressed to Rome, others forwarded from Naples, but none bearing a date more recent than the 5th. At dinner this evening we found ourselves among a host of English, and marvelled at the absence of the Trans-Atlantic accent, till we were told that the Americans were all at the other table. There are two long tables, and such is the extreme delicacy of the Landlord's perceptions that he 'spots' the nationality of his guests at once, and arranges them accordingly. The English and Americans divide the hotel pretty equally between them, leaving very little space for other nations.

We are extremely comfortable here, and are heartily sorry to leave the Russie. Every night Perrini doses me with some 'medicine' which he prepares for me himself, and which consists of brandy, yolk of egg, sugar, hot water, &c and though it sounds horrible, it is really most delicious.

Thursday, 13 February. As we were coming down stairs to go out, we met Mrs. Hartley just coming in to call on us, but she would not detain us, so we went on our way, and took a carriage to drive about and get a general idea of the ancient part of the city. In this one morning's drive we saw so many glorious 'monuments of antiquity' (to use the guide-book phrase) that our brains grow almost bewildered in thinking of them all, but we hope to see them all again and again, to revisit each one till its form grows a familiar friend to our eye, and the spirit of its history sinks into our heart. First there was the Capitol with its splendid old piazza, and that glorious bronze equestrian statue of Hadrian. Hard by, in the church of S. Maria we saw the dwelling place of *il sanctissimo bambino,* but the precious relic itself was not at home, in fact we met it on the steps, being carried in its box to a handsome carriage and pair, with two footmen, that stood at the foot of the steps. This was the carriage of Prince Torlonia, who, being ill, had sent for the miraculous bambino to come and cure him! In the courtyard of the Palace of the Conservatori on the opposite side of the Piazza, we saw some of the 'wild' horses or 'barberi' from which the Carnival racers were to be selected, and a brilliant set they were, all old and *passé,* though well-bred; one especially attracted our notice, as it could only go on three legs! From the Capitol we descended to the Forum, and watched the Excavations going on there with much interest. The Basilica Julia, the fine arch of Septimus Severus, the Three Columns of the Temple of Vespasian (so familiar to us long before on brooches) the Portico of the Twelve Gods, and the column of Phocas, all close together, claimed our attention, and then we went on to the Palace of the Caesars, on Mons Palatinus, a series of vaulted chambers, recently excavated, above which is a terrace with a very fine view. We went in to the little Museum, of antiquities and relics found in the Caesars' palace, amphora, busts, glass vessels become iridescent by long burial, &c &c. Among the busts was one very fine one of Augustus, strikingly like the Great Napoleon, and a little head that took our fancy greatly, from its expression of intense comicality and joviality, so natural, and real that one *could not help* smiling in response. From this most interesting view we went down to the splendid arch of Titus, with its famous bas-reliefs, the brazen candlestick in the procession of the Captive Jews so *very* familiar, and the whole so often seen in engravings that one seemed to know it well already. Then we went on to the noble, much larger, but less ancient, Arch of Constantine, and admired it immensely, and *then,* to the Colosseum. It is glorious, magnificent; it raised us to a pitch of enthusiasm, that nothing, save S. Peters, had ever done before. The grey arches stood out nobly against the dark blue sky, and the whole effect was not alone grand and majestic, but also most wondrously beautiful. The only thing that I wished different, was the inner space of the Arena,

which is in my opinion, sadly marred by the presence of
numerous wretched little shrines – 'stations', I suppose, with
tawdry paintings, painfully out of place amid the solemn
grandeur of the Colosseum, which without them, would be
perfect. It is essentially *pagan,* a survival of the *old* Roman
religion, and these appendages of the degraded Christianity of
the *modern* Roman religion, are woefully incongruous.

From the Colosseum we drove to the famous Church of St.
John Lateran, which delighted us immensely, especially the
Corsini Chapel. This we 'did' more thoroughly than we have
yet done anything in Rome, gazing at the exquisite statues
with which it is adorned, and descending to the crypt beneath
to see the beautiful Pieta, Bernini's great work, a group of the
most exquisite delicacy and beauty. We then went to the Scala
Sancta, and saw there three men wearily climbing up it on
their knees, in the hope of indulgence, or as an act of penance.
And now our morning's work was over, and we drove back to
the Russie to lunch. After that we transferred ourselves and
our belongings to our new quarters, and then went for a stroll
on the Pincian, with which we are charmed.

At five we took a most recherché Victoria we saw in the
Piazza, with silver mountings, showy horse, *very* showy driver,
quite a dazzling little turn-out (compare with our London
cabs, and confess the superiority of Rome!), and drove to the
Mamertine Prison, which was specially lighted up, we were
told. Our driver stopped in a small square filled with carriages
evidently waiting for their occupants. We got out, and as our
driver told us to go straight on, we wandered on, seeing
nothing at all like an entrance to a prison or to anything at all,
but pointed onwards by the men, who all seemed to know
what we wanted without our appealing to them, till we came
to what looked like the back way to a mews. Here we did
hesitate, but the numerous ostlers and coachmen about said we
were all right, and we went on, through a little door, and

down a dark passage till we suddenly found ourselves in the midst of a large party of English and American tourists, all carrying torches, and listening to a sort of lecture which Mr. Parker (whom Dearman knows) was giving. To them we joined ourselves, and we all went through the five vaults of the prison, where Jugurtha and Catiline, and St. Paul were, almost certainly, confined, and, tradition says, St. Peter also. From the main part of the prison to St. Peter's cell, we had to go down a narrow low little passage just like a drain, and more than 100 yards long, which, creeping slowly along, almost on hands and knees, as we were, seemed *interminable,* and was most fearfully hot and stifling. The laughter and merriment with which it was entered, soon changed into silence, or groans, or gasps, or anxious inquiries, 'Shall we have to come back the same way, Mr Parker?' &c. This passage much resembles a drain in size and form, and has only just now been discovered and cleared. When at last we emerged, we found ourselves in the cell said to be Peter's, and we all drank out of the well which sprang up miraculously in order to enable him to baptize his jailors, and then we slowly made our way, up and up, out into the fresh air of heaven once more, having been nearly asphyxiated, but immensely interested.

After dinner we paid a most delightful moonlight visit to the Colosseum, and most glorious it was, but the lovely evening had drawn thither numbers of tourists, and their voices and laughter were so little in harmony with the noble silence of the great still amphitheatre, and one heartily wished them all away, it was so entirely a case where 'only man was vile'.

From the Colosseum we went to the Pantheon, but found it all locked up for the night; however, on going round to the back, we succeeded in finding the sacristan, an old monk, who admitted us. He was by no means remarkable for symmetry of feature, a fact which Perrini instantly observed, and when we

were absorbed in the contemplation of the large dimly-lighted
mysterious-seeming rotunda, he drew our attention to the
shadow of light cast by the moon on the interior of the dome;
'Oh! how very remarkable! look sir, how wonderfully like the
profile of the old monkey at the door! What a strange
coincidence! I will call him, that you may see for yourselves.'
He then proceeded to go back for the monk, and returned with
him, politely asking him something about the church in
Italian, and then turning to us, just as if translating the holy
man's answer, and gravely saying 'Now sir, you see the
resemblance I spoke of. Look at the nose of this rascally old
monkey, and observe how exact its portrait. Then too the chin'
– but at this point we were both compelled to turn our backs
precipitately on the monk and bury ourselves and our mirth in
the dark recesses of the church. Perrini's absolute
imperturbability of visage, and the calm way in which he
alternately does the polite on such occasions, to the priests, in
Italian, and then abuses them to us in English, are a constant
trial to our gravity. His hatred to the priests is something
tremendous, and he seems to have seen a good deal of their
dark side. He told us a story of one in Jerusalem, whom he
exposed. He was travelling with a Roman Catholic family, and
they ordered him to take the Communion and confess himself,
in their presence. This he objected to, as he did not believe in
Roman Catholicism but he found nothing else would satisfy
them, so he went to the priest, and told him the
circumstances. The priest at first refused to have anything to
do with it, whereon Perrini hinted that his master had
entrusted him with £50 for the church. The priest, snatching
at the idea, immediately became anxious to make terms with
him, and proposed to arrange the matter thus: Perrini should
come to the Confessional, kneel down, and have a little chat
with him, while appearing to confess to him. He, (the priest)
would then *seem* to give him the bread of the Communion

without really doing so. To this plan Perrini assented, in order to see how far the priest's cupidity would lead him. The farce was gone through, the family were satisfied, and the priest gave Perrini a written certificate that he had confessed and taken the Communion, signed with the seal of Jerusalem, but then, when the holy Father eagerly claimed the £50, Perrini told him it was all a hoax, winding up with 'If you are so ready to cheat God, you deserve that I should cheat you.' The priests at Jerusalem and in the Holy Land generally seem more thoroughly debased than they do anywhere else.

We had an amusing scene at dinner. Very near us sat two American ladies, very lively and pleasant, the elder looking about 35, the younger about 20. It appeared that they were mother and daughter, though they hardly looked like it, and they were talking to a German lady opposite them, and describing some man who had persisted in repeating 'No, it is your niece, Madam, you are mistaken, it cannot be your daughter'. Whereon a very solemn old Scotchman who sat between them and us began to address the ambient air (we suppose – for he looked at nobody, but straight before him) in an almost sepulchral tone: 'The American climate is early destructive to female beauty; American women are the most beautiful in the world, but they fade before their time, and daughters frequently look older than their mothers.' 'Then I suppose you think I look older than mama?' 'Well, like her sister, we will say. Understand me, I think American women the most beautiful in the world, but the American climate is early destructive.' 'Oh! dear, I am sure I will never go back to America then, do you think if I were to stay in England, it might put me back a few years?' 'If you were to stay in England, my dear lady, you would soon be as comely and well-favoured as your Mother.'

During all this conversation, which was prolonged for some time in the same strain, we were all in convulsions of laughter, but the old gentleman went on the even tenor of his way, in his solemn discourse, seeming quite unconscious of the cachinnations around him. He is quite alone, and rarely speaks, so that one forgets his presence, and his sepulchral voice takes one by surprise.

Friday, 14 February. A very quiet day, compared with the preceding. Dearman called on Major Allen the first thing, and then we both went to call on Mrs. Hartley, and had a long chat with her and two of her widow companions. In the afternoon she went with us for a lovely drive to the Villa Pamfili Doria, whence we had a most glorious panoramic view, as it occupies the summit of the Janiculum. The gardens too are very charming and the day was most perfect. Major Allen came to dine with us (at the *Table d'hôte*) and stayed all the evening. There are about 40 at dinner, always much the same party, and they seem very nice people; the German lady next to us is particularly pleasant and nice.

Saturday, 15 February. Yes, she certainly is; and the American ladies, Mrs. and Miss Courtenay, are nice too, and evidently belong to the very best class of Americans, but still the constant song of my grateful heart is the same.

> 'I thank the goodness and the grace
> That on my birth hath smiled
> I was born no Yankee or German
> But a happy English child.'

This sweet poem runs in my head unceasingly, and I would fain give it vent in song, but 'I am saddest when I sing, and so are those that hear me.'

This first day of Carnival has been a very lively opportunity. One has so often read of the wild merriment of the Farewell to the Flesh, that it is pleasant to be in the very thick of it oneself. We have taken a balcony for the eight days, and think ourselves fortunate to have got it for £16 (400 francs). It is just below the Via Condotti, in a very good part of the Corso. We had made a resolution not to throw any confetti this first day, so although I had some secret longing to engage in the fray, we retaliated not one whit, and bore meekly (through our wire sceeens) all the fire that was levelled against us. I was considerably pelted, both with confetti and with bouquets, twice by no humbler and assailant than Prince Arthur[12] himself, who seemed to be enjoying the fun immensely, enveloped in brown holland. Major Allen was with us in our balcony. We took our places at two, and the confetti throwing very soon began. At three there was a grand procession. Horses gaily caparisoned, and ridden by young Italian nobles (*on dit*) in the most gorgeous array, cars symbolical or historical in character. Bands of music and mounted *gens d'armes*. At five the streets were cleared by the National Guard and at 5.30 the 23 'barberi' or wild, riderless horses, let free to gallop down the whole length of the Corso, their departure and arrival being announced by guns, and before six we made our way home.

I was greatly edified this morning by Dearman's skill in playing the housemaid. Before I was dressed he was hard at work in our sitting room, and when I came in to breakfast, he led me round the room, pointing out, with commendable pride, all the reforms he had effected. The books (our library mainly consists of red hand-books!) were artistically disposed on our one marble table; the newspapers carefully arranged on the top shelf of the what-not, the second shelf being adorned with my workbag as a centrepiece, the pendants to it being the opera-glass and a solitary *pear!* Cloaks, shawls and coats were

---

[12] A son of Queen Victoria, born in 1850, so two years older than Emily. He was afterwards Duke of Connaught.

all folded up in a pile, which was crowned by my muff. The ink-stand had one table all to itself, our pen-holders being dextrously placed in a square around it; the chairs were all solemnly disposed, against the wall, all round the room, and the umbrellas reposed on the window seat. Altogether the room was in a state of such severe orderliness that one felt one could scarcely enter it without desecration.

We have a waiter here who interests us deeply; he looks as if he had had a history, as if he 'was somebody', and conjectures the most romantic are rife respecting him. He looks (and says) as if he had lost a dynasty, I say, as if he were some prince in disguise. He has a sort of 'ancien régime' appearance, with his white hair, lofty forehead, black eyebrows, fiery black eyes, straight nose, well-cut mouth and chin, and heavy iron grey moustache. And he is so *intensely* solemn and stately. He dosen't understand a word of English, and yet Dearman will persist in discoursing to him in that language, much to his discomfiture. This is rather a way Dearman has, and no representations will induce him to abandon what seems to me so aimless a course. He defends it, by saying that his hearers are just as pleased as if they understood. For instance, the other day, when we were driving to Spezzia, Dearman walked a great part of the way, and a man shewed him several short cuts, and accompanied him, and they had much agreeable conversation. The man would hold forth for some time in very patois-Italian, and then Dearman would thank him very politely for his pleasing remarks and interesting information, whereat the man always seemed greatly gratified, and this performance was repeated several times, both of them on the best possible terms with the other, and in a very friendly and amiable frame of mind, and neither of them understanding one word that the other had said.

This morning we received the news of the birth of my youngest little niece, Lily's second daughter. It is most extraordinary that we should not have heard of it before, for the infant is a week old today, and even now we only hear of it through a casual remark in a letter from F. who only mentions it after writing 3 pages on other subjects. The slowness of the post between England and Italy is something wonderful.

Sunday, 16 February. In the morning we went to the English church, outside the Porta del Popolo. It was *crowded,* and we heard that many were obliged to go away, unable to find even standing room. Prince Arthur was there, and the sermon was preached by Archbishop French, whom I delighted to have the opportunity of hearing, and who gave us an exceedingly good sermon.

After lunch we walked about on the Pincio, which was extremely gay. We saw the Princess Margharita driving in semi-state, Prince Arthur walking among the crowd, and the King driving in a very simple Victoria, recognized only by the raising of English hats, and keeping the line just like all the other carriages.

Monday, 17 February. Dearman's cold, which had been pretty bad on Saturday, and worse on Sunday, was still worse today, and made his head so bad that he resolved to try some strong remedy, and decided on taking a Turkish bath. He went off for this purpose at 12, having previously entrusted me to Mrs. Hartley, and arranged for me to see the Carnival from her window, as he did not like me to go to our balcony without him. I spent the afternoon with Mrs. Hartley and her friend Signora Ugolinucci, a *charming* Roman lady, and returned home at 5.30. I found Dearman looking very white and poorly, and heard to my horror that in my absence he had an exceedingly narrow escape. It appears that these Turkish bath people do not understand their business at all, for after various small discomforts and misadventures, Dearman was

actually nearly suffocated by the fumes of charcoal which they
had put on the fire in large quantities, and as the chimney was
too small, a great part of the smoke came into the room – a
wretched little cell to begin with. He did not quite lose
consciousness, but was extremely ill, convulsive motions all
over, gasping for breath, and then extreme prostration. The
people were excessively frightened, sent for a doctor, and put
him to bed for two hours, after which about 4 p.m. he
returned home. Mrs. Hartley came and dined with us in our
salon, and Dearman could eat no dinner, and seemed weak and
faint, all the evening, so by Mrs. Hartley's advice we sent for a
very nice Scotch doctor, Gregor by name, who gave him some
medicine, advised him to go to bed, and thought he would
soon be all right, but was most indignant with the bath-
people, and said it had been a most narrow escape. Dearman
thinks the bath really did him good, in spite of all, for it seems
to have cured his cold. He has taken almost no food, during
the entire day. There was actually not even a thermometer in
this wretched so-called Turkish bath. It is certainly a lesson
against trying experiments of this kind in a foreign land.

Tuesday, 18 February.   Dearman slept well, and was very
much better this morning, quite like himself, indeed. He
enjoyed his breakfast, and told me to go out in the sun, but
not to go to our balcony. We therefore lent the latter to the
Goodriches, whom Dearmen met on Sunday, and who called
here yesterday. I went with Mrs. Hartley to have my hair cut
this morning. Yesterday she took me to have my ears pierced,
which seemed an operation mysteriously difficult to accom-
plish, for we applied in vain at several jewellers' shops, and at
last were conducted by a very nice jeweller whom Mrs. H.
knew, to an old woman up about 8 flights of stairs, who
proceeded to do one, but couldn't manage the other, my ears
were 'so fat!' so the man did that one himself. They put the

rings in at once, without first doing them with a needle. My ears are considerably 'took' (as F. would say) today, but I am glad the ceremony is over.

This afternoon we have been generally strolling about on the Pincio, watching the models (?) dance on the Spanish steps, and poking about at several of the Cameo and mosaic shops, taking a general survey, before committing ourselves to any purchases. We have dined in our own salon.

This morning we received a Leeds Mercury of January 30th, addressed to Rome, and a Times of 13th February, sent round by Nice.

Wednesday, 19 February. By far the best day of the Carnival so far. No confetti thrown, only bouquets and real sweetmeats. In the morning, after a call from Mrs. Hartley, we went for a walk along the via Sebastiana, past the baths of Caracalla, then round to the Colosseum and so home through the Forum. After lunch we repaired to our balcony, and spent a most pleasant afternoon there, Mrs. Hartley being with us.

The processions were most gorgeous, and the costumes far more splendid than on the confetti throwing days. Besides the same triumphal and symbolical cars as we saw on the previous days, there was a long series of pageants, one representing Charles V and his court, mounted on beautiful horses, and arrayed with the greatest magnificence, another being a train of lords and ladies out hawking, real falcons tied to their wrists; then came a miniature war-steamer, then a hunt with dogs and deer, and keepers with hares and partridges slung around them, and the huntsmen in scarlet on horseback; then a procession of 50 horses, some mounted by superbly clad riders, others led by men dressed as Arabs, Turks, Chinese, Circassians, Armenians, &c.; then an old lady of the last century, with powdered hair, patches on her face, hoops and brocades, in a Sedan chair, carried by bearers in appropriate

costumes. This last masquerade attracted so much admiration
and attention, that the chair was several times stopped, unable
to make its way through the dense crowd.

There were hosts of people in masquerading attire, besides
those in carriages or on horseback, and some of the costumes
were most amusing. Three *pelicans,* with white plumage and
long beaks, rushed about, cackling and pecking at the
bystanders; others had heads of elephants, or monkeys, or
foolscaps, or masks of the most hideous grotesqueness, and one
great big man had a fat round smiling baby's face. A long thin
figure in flowing white garments, with white mask over his
eyes, and long white nose, but the mouth left uncovered, came
and made love to me in dumb show, in the most charmingly
graceful and refined way, and with the most touching
raisemblance, and when I at last bestowed some bonbons,
bowed low in his gratitude, and then laying his hand on his
heart lamented that he had *nothing but that* to offer me! We hear
that the poor old pope was direfully offended by one of the
Symbolical cars, which was surmounted by a parrot in a cage,
standing on the dome of S. Peter's, and with a white flag
waving over it. The parrot typified His Holiness, the 'prisoner
of the Vatican', and the flag, the ensign of the Comte de
Chambord, signified the protection of his interests by the
Legitimist party in France.

This evening we dined at the *Table d'hôte,* the first time for 2
days, and we were disgusted to find that our places had been
filled up, and that we were consigned to a little side-table!

Thursay, 20 February. The dinner-table affair has been
happily adjusted; we told Perrini the state of the case, and it
was as if we had applied a match to a train of gunpowder. At
our first word he fired up, and bolted off to the landlord, for he
always waxes wrath where he thinks the dignity of 'his family'
is affronted: 'You put my family at a little table like two

children! I can tell you *my* family will not stand that' and
pitched into them with such effect that he gained his point,
and the waiter told me afterwards that they had used all
efforts, *'on a fait l'impossible'* and our place was restored.

We had a most glorious walk this morning, taking with us
no guide or companion but our invaluable map, and finding
our way to the Porta S. Paolo by all sorts of curious and
interesting ways and by-paths, coming upon many quaint and
amusing scenes that we should never meet with, were we to
drive about in a carriage, or to be led from place to place by
courier or cicerone. Altogether we like our plan immensely,
and we both enjoy the long independent rambles to the full.
Today we had a particularly delightful one. I was guide, as I
had traced our route beforehand on the map, and I succeeded
most beautifully in making my way through a most interesting part of the town, past all kinds of historic scenes (of
which more anon) to our desired goal. The only drawback was
that Dearman was disgracefully sceptical, and critical, and
shewed an amount of bad taste I had not supposed him capable
of, in being unpleasantly wide-awake, and drawing attention
to various little facts which I was striving to ignore, such for
instance, as the circumstance that in my effort to find the
nearest way, we had walked through one street (the Via del
Tor di Specchi – I should know it again, even if I met with it
in Kamschatka *three times;* and on another such occasion he
remarked with singular want of tact, 'Oh! here's our old friend
the Theatre of Marcellus again; we passed him ten minutes
ago'. However, even 'the disaffected member' was obliged to
bite the dust, and acknowledge that I had led him by the best
possible way, for in our third promenade along that horrid
Specchi street, we somehow (why, I don't exactly know) dived
up a little yard, and suddenly found ourselves close in front of
the rock Tarpeian, which was really thrilling. We had strayed
into the private premises of a Roman Washerwoman, and

clothes hung in white lines all round us, but there was *the* rock, and nothing could mar our pleasure in gazing on it.

We had before this been much interested by the grand old Portico di Octavia, where the Fishmarket is, and by many wonderful old arches or antique houses, with beautiful ancient cornices which came upon us at every turn. From the Rupe Tarpeia we went on, through the Piazza della Bocca di Verita, past the Temple of Vesta, then along by the base of the beautiful Aventine, with its warm-tinted ruined walls, its stone-pines, and its vineyards, till we came to the edge of the Tiber, and there I saw just below, the remains of an *old bridge.* My heart leaped for a sure instinct told me 'that must be all that is left of the Bridge of Horatius!' It was this that I had longed to see, more perhaps than anything else in Rome. I had read it up in Murray, and found it there prosaically called the Sublician bridge, so now, when I think I see its foundations before my eyes I wish to make assurance doubly sure; and before giving free course to my emotions, I make a desperate effort to rally the scattered forces of my Italian vocabulary, I arrange a sentence in hot haste, I rush to the guardhouse, dash open the door, and find myself in the midst of a body of soldiery, at whom I discharge my volley *'E quello il ponte Sublicio, vi prego di dirmi?'* The 'captain of the gate' (a stalwart youth, successor to Horatius) steps forward, and replies politely *'Si, signora, il ponte di Horatio.'* I nearly faint at the words, I gasp out a syllable of thanks, I dart out again. I lean over the low wall, I look down on the basements of the piers of Rome's oldest bridge, I look up and across the 'broad floods' to the 'further shore' where brave Horatius stood alone and where the thrice thirty thousand, all Etrurias noblest shrank back 'from the ghastly entrance where those bold Romans stood,' I gaze on the yellow river, as tawny now as then, my feet are on the very spot where 'now he feels the bottom, now on dry earth he stands,' and the grand heroism of twenty four hundred years ago seems clear and real before my eyes. At last I tore myself away from this classic spot, and we pursued our way, past ruined palaces, and bright modern gardens, under ancient arches, and through beautiful avenues, till we saw on our right a singular-looking hill, no great height, but standing alone and therefore commanding a very fine view, as we found when we reached the top (for we could not resist the temptation to turn aside and ascend it). This proved to be the Monte Testaccio, a hill entirely composed of broken pots, as to the origin of which antiquarians are hopelessly puzzled. Then we went on past the Protestant cemetery, to Porta S. Paola, and then took another road homewards, over the other shoulder of the Aventine, and so, past the Circus Maximus to the Colosseum and the Forum.

The afternoon was spent in our balcony, where we both of us returned with vigour all the fire of confetti, and bouquets that was levelled at us. (The *bon-bons* that rained upon me, I took care *not* to return; *they* were safely consigned to my pocket!) This was an extremely busy day on the Corso.

Friday, 21 February. A 'dies non,' as far as King Carnival is concerned; the Roman Times in its programme for the week devotes Friday to 'headaches and rest'. We didn't have headaches, and we didn't rest particularly, but we enjoyed the day immensely. In the morning we took another delicious walk, Dearman being guide this time, and as I am flushed with the brilliant success of yesterday, I can afford to be generous, and will therefore do him the justice to say that he found his way, without one false step, and gave us a most charming and interesting walk. (This much, fairness to him compels me to say, but like Galileo, I add my saving clause under my breath: 'all the same it was *not* equal to *my* walk, and *my bridge!*')

Again we had a superb day, bright and hot in the sun, with delightful breeze. We went up the Spanish steps, along the Via Sistina and Via Felice, past the Palazzo Barbarini, and the

Quattro Fontane, to S. Maria Maggiore, which we visited, and we also went into the church of S. Praxedis, (daughter of Pudens – a lady whose name was strange to me till I came to Rome, I blush to say –). We went on as far as the church of S.S. Peter and Marcellus, when we turned to the left, out of the Via Merulana into the Via Labicana, a nice quiet country lane, between hedges and high green banks, which led us to the grand Porta Maggiore, at the beginning of the splendid Claudian Aqueduct. From this, the finest of the gates of Rome, we went to the church of S. Croce in Jerusalemme, and thence to S. Giovanni in Laterano, whence the view that lovely morning was most enchanting. After lunch at Spillmans – such a charming shop, by the way; Dearman has his heart's desire in a monotonous daily repetition of oysters and porter, while *I,* with my usual delicate refinement of taste, revel in cakes, meringues, chocolate creams, and curaçoa. Well, after lunch we drove to the church of S. Paul's without the Walls, a *most gorgeous* edifice, very large, the next in size to S. Peter's, and very very rich, in mosaics and marbles, altars of solid malachite, lovely mosaic medallions of all the popes round the walls, massive pillars of the rarest marble, etc. etc. From this splendid church (modern) we drove on to the Tre Fontane, the supposed scene of S. Paul's martyrdom, where a monastery and 3 churches have been built. In one of these churches are the three fountains that sprang miraculously from the blood from Paul's head, which made 3 leaps in falling, and also the broken pillar that served as the block.

A French monk shewed us round, and gave us a deplorable account of the deadly unhealthiness of the place in summer. It is absolutely impossible for any human being to sleep there in July and August, and all the monks always suffer from fever from being there merely in the day-time.

Major Allen called in the evening, and we went out for a stroll with him.

Saturday, 22 February. On this morning, Dearman being fired with an ardent desire to cross the Tiber in a ferry, and then to walk through the fields of Quintus Cincinnatus, we resolved to carry this romantic sounding plan into execution. We found our way, down the Via Ripetta, to the ferry, and beheld there an enormous boat, as big as a house, and really nearly filling up the whole of the river, so that our voyage was by no means a hazardous one, in fact so slowly did the monster pass over the few yards that separated its prow from the further shore, that I was not aware we were moving at all, till I perceived that our few fellow passengers were landing. And then came the question of payment, and we offered the man five francs, but he had no change, so would not accept it, and we promised to come back the same way, and pay him then, which *I* faithfully intended to do though I afterwards found that Dearman had never seriously purposed it in his heart! The end of it is that we came back quite another way, and the debt is still unpaid, and lies a heavy burden on my conscience. True, it is but *'due soldi'* for the two, but 'the principle of the thing' is the same. I was rather at a loss to understand Dearman's intense enthusiasm for Cincinnatus for he quite raved about that worthy, and during the whole of our walk went into ecstasies at every step, rehearsing to me every instant the story of the old gentleman digging his turnips, and – but I need not repeat it again, *I* may spare *myself,* at any rate, though really, the facts have been lately so frequently impressed on my mind that they almost force their way into my journal. The story is, of course, very thrilling on first acquaintance, but after the 10th time of repetition it begins to grow monotonous. However, to Dearman it afforded intense delight, and though I saw 'nothing but a very prosaic footpath, between high walls most of the way, the fact that it ran through Q.C.'s very garden made it classic ground in his eyes, though I fancy he was secretly disappointed to find no ruined walls to mark

the spot where stood that historic hovel, no relics of the Great
Agriculturist, no inscription even, no eager native to rush
forth and solemnly bid us 'behold the Home of Quintus
Cincinnatus'. (How tired I am of the old fellow's name!) As I
said, this *extreme* ardour was perplexing to my colder mind, till
the suspicion crossed me, that it was, in great part, assumed as
a sort of retaliation for my enthusiasm of the day before at the
bridge of Horatius. Be this as it may through these fields we
walked, behind the Castle of S. Angelo, to S. Peter's, and on
our way, we were much edified by watching the manoeuvres of
a portion of the Army of Italy. One party of nice-looking boys
(very raw recruits) was being instructed in the noble art of
jumping over a skipping-rope, in performing which feat they
everyone of them tumbled headlong; others were learning to
vault, and it certainly was the most shuffling, scrambling,
climbing operation I ever saw in my life.

Another party were being taught to dig trenches, which
they did in the usual style of the Italians, taking about a
thimbleful of earth in the spade at once, and resting five
minutes between every flourish of the spade.

In coming out of S. Peter's this morning, who should we
fall in with, but our friend *Cantini,* with a party! He stopped
and spoke to us, and explained his presence there, by stating
that he had just arrived from England, having finished his
'important private business' earlier than he expected and
therefore taken advantage of an engagement that offered itself
just at the right time! It was a rather amusing rencontre.

After lunch we repaired to our balcony and engaged in the
usual warfare there. The Corso was not quite so busy as on
Thursday though in the neighbourhood on the Royal Balcony
(where Prince Arthur and the Princess Margherita were
extremely active and energetic) the crowd was *dense* the whole
afternoon. At five o'clock we ventured out, and braved the
storm by walking up the Corso to Mrs. Hartley's, where we

went to see the horses start from the Piazzo del Popolo. We played bezique in the evening, and I made 800, Dearman 80!! He had beaten me hollow the night before.

Sunday, 23 February.   In the morning we went to church, and found it as crowded as last Sunday. Mr. Carter of Clewer, preached and gave us a capital sermon. After church we took a walk in the Borghese gardens, then lunched at Spillman's, and then went again to church, and heard Mr. Grant, the chaplain. We then went for a stroll on the Pincio, which was extremely gay, with Mmes. Hartley and Lacy, and saw the King several times. He was driving in state. We wound up the afternoon by going to hear the nuns sing, at the Trinita di Monte. The singing was very sweet and pretty, but we both thought that, as a performance, it had been over-rated, being always spoken of as one of the 'things to be done' in Rome.

Monday, 24 February.   A very pretty fancy fair was opened yesterday in the Piazza di Spagna, and in the evening we strolled through it, greatly enjoying the splendid military band, and admiring the orderliness of the large crowd, of people of all classes. The square is hung with festoons of evergreens, from which are suspended hundreds of Chinese lanterns, alternately red and white, which, when lighted have an exceedingly pretty effect. Today we did not go to the Carnival at all, but lent our balcony to the Ugolinucci family. In the meantime, we had a most charming day driving in the morning (Mmes. Hartley and Lacy accompanying us) to the wonderful tombs in the Via Latina, which are certainly among the most interesting sights of Rome. One of them especially, the tomb of Pancratius, amazed and delighted us beyond measure by the marvellous preservation, and exceeding beauty, of its decorations. The roof and walls of the vault were painted in red and green, the colours as deep and fresh as possible, picked out with white, and with the most lovely white medallions, and all kinds of designs *astounding* us by their grace and clearness. As a triumph of decorative art, it was admirable, even apart from its antiquarian interest. From the tombs, we drove on for some distance, alongside of the beautiful remains of the Claudian aqueduct, which are ruined in the picturesquest possible way, and partly overgrown with ivy, forming a charming foreground to one of the most enchanting views in the world, the lovely Alban Hills being its background. We returned to Rome by the Appian Way, which we must explore more thoroughly another day. This afternoon we have been strolling about for three hours, visiting the ghastly, grotesque, but curious, interesting, and certainly unique, cemetery below the church of the Capuchins, which is decorated entirely with the bones of departed monks, all arranged in fantastic patterns, while others, more recently taken up from the holy earth of Jerusalem, in which each one rests only till his place is wanted for another, stand in niches, fully dressed and bearing in their withered hands their crucifix and rosary. The bones of 5000 dead Capuchins repose – no, anything but *repose,* to be set up and exposed to the gaze of the curious to the end of time – have their abode here, and one wonders at the coolness with which the living ones, habited exactly like those brown skeletons in the niches, can gaze on their dead brethren, whose fate must, sooner or later, be theirs. From this weird necropolis we rambled along the Via del Quirinale to the Royal Palace, admired the fine statues in the Piazza, which bear the (surely false?) inscriptions 'Opus Phidiae' and 'Opus Praxitelis' respectively, then entered the Colonna Gardens, from the terrace of which we had a splendid view of Rome, and where are the ancient Baths of Constantine. We then walked to S. Maria Maggiore, and all through the new boulevard, where whole terraces of large

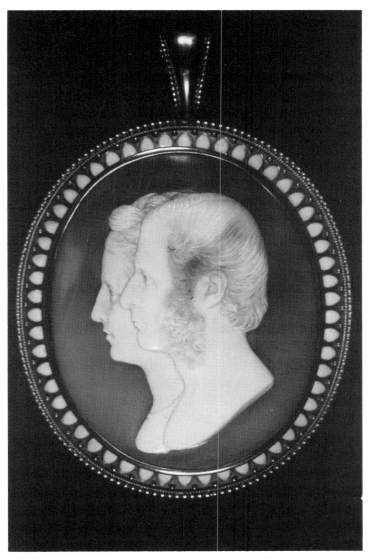

Cameo of Dearman and Emily by Sanchi of Rome, 1873

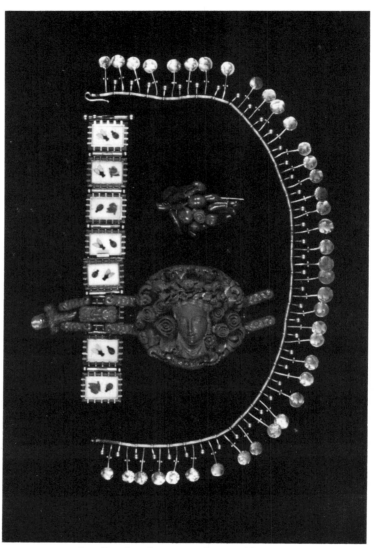

Jewellry bought on Emily's wedding tour

houses are being built. Somehow we had always fancied Rome
a city of of the past, and it was a fresh light on the subject to
see this flourishing district, with its building operations on so
extensive a scale. We found out the Hotel Costangi, and went
in to spy out the land. The drawing, reading, and billiard
rooms are charming, but one part of the new wing is but just
finished, and the whole hotel struck us as damp and not very
desirable at present, though in a few years' time it will no
doubt be delightful. We finished our walk by a stroll on the
Pincian, watching the sun set in a blaze of glory behind S.
Peter's.

Tuesday, 25 February.   Mrs. Hartley called at 10, and then
she and we went on a shopping expedition, our principal visit
being to Castellani's most charming studio. We were greatly
admiring, and my soul was greatly coveting some most lovely
gold and mosaic imitations of early Etruscan jewellery, and
when Mr. Castellani came up, we ventured to ask the price of
some of these treasures, and were deeply grieved to find that
they were none of them for sale, being merely a sort of
museum for *chefs d'oeuvre* specially dear to their maker's heart.
He took us into another room, where were the things that were
to be bought, and Dearman selected a lovely little set, brooch
and earrings, to give me. The value of the things seemed to my
uninitiated mind, extraordinary. I wanted some pretty, simple, gold bracelets for presents, and seeing a most lovely one,
chaste, refined, and most delicately and exquisitely worked,
but not large or massive, and with no stone or mosaic work, I
asked the value of it. 'Sixteen months' workmanship' replied
Mr. Castellani, and on being requested to express himself in
terms more suited to our comprehension, he calmly said '120
guineas'. Each article he has in his shop is a real work of art.
   This being the last day of Carnival, the Corso was extremely
gay when we took our places on our balcony, about 3 p.m.

Mrs. Hartley and Mme. Lefèvre, a young Frenchwoman whom she knows, were with us, also Major Allen part of the time. The masked figures were more numerous than ever, and some of them most grotesque, little men hiding their insignificance in *huge* heads, boys dressed as women, and women as boys, the bloomer costume being a great favourite, ladies prettily dressed as contadine, men by the score in sailors' costume, one carriage-ful of gentlemen encased in black, fitting tight to their bodies, with tails, and monkeys faces, others attired as nuns and monks, even the ghastly looking 'Frati della Misericordia', whose grim office it is to bury the dead, being parodied in their long sacking garments, their faces entirely concealed and only holes, pierced for their eyes. A miniature war-steamer, the funnel smoking all properly, manned by a gallant young crew, was very pretty, and so was a Swiss chalet, both these of course on wheels, and drawn by horses. The car of Pasquino was a very gorgeous affair, decorated with flags, evergreens, and flowers, with magnificently dressed ladies seated on it, and in the middle, high above, a huge broken eggshell, within which stood King Pasquino himself in flowing white, with a memorable beard, and bowing graciously in acknowledgement of the bouquets that were showered upon him. Many of the horses, even, that took part in the procession, were painted with stripes of various colours, and their heads of course gaily adorned with rosettes and flowers.

After the usual 'Corsa dei Barberi' the carriages came back into the Corso (they are always ordered off before the race), and from six to seven the Moccoletti fun reigned supreme. The effect of the gay illuminations, the whole length of the Corso was most charming, and the procession, with the triumphal cars brilliant with coloured lights, looked like a scene from fairyland. Each house was a blaze of light, and everyone carried in his hand a torch or taper, or more ambitiously, a Bengal light.

The universal view of course was to keep one's own light burning, and to extinguish that of everybody else, and those unfortunates whose candles had been put out were assailed with shouts of *'Senza moccolo'* until they relighted them. All this we had heard and read of, but never realized till then.

We dined at 7.30 (the *Table d'hôte* paying reference to the Moccoletti) and immediately after dinner we went to the Apollo where we had taken a box, from which to witness the last grand masquerade of the Carnival. Major Allen was our only guest, and we had a very pleasant evening. There was hardly any dancing, merely a crowded promenade, but the general effect was extremely pretty, and it was a very amusing sight. All the ladies were masked, and most of them in costume; some of the gentlemen were dressed in character, but the majority just in evening dress, and many of them even wore their hats! There were no end of English.

Wednesday, 26 February. Ash Wednesday, and Carnival all over. Lent has begun very quietly indeed for us. We went to church this morning and found a very good congregation, Mr Grant preaching the sermon. Then we had a little stroll with Mrs Hartley, then lunch at our inestimable Spillman's and then a quiet afternoon, writing letters. We were quite intending to go to Naples today, but have received no answer whatever from the telegram Perrini has sent in turn to the H. de Russie and to the Grande Bretagne. We suppose Naples is quite full, so shall just wait here till we hear we can have rooms. Prince Arthur and the King have gone there today.

Thursday, 27 February. This morning we went to the Capitol, to look down on the Tarpeian Rock, from above, and then to the Palazzo dei Conservatori, where we fell in with the Courtenays, who were most friendly, and took us in their carriage to Spillman's, where we all lunched together. Again we spent a quiet afternoon, for Dearman is not very well, and felt inclined to rest, and I was by no means sorry to have time for writing. Still no news from Naples; it is rather unsettling to go on putting off going there from day to day, but we are in such good quarters here that we need not complain. Dearman is just now deeply absorbed in Transformation; he thinks it the most charming book he ever read.

Friday, 28 February.   Dearman is better, but not well yet, so this morning he stayed quietly in the house, whilst I went (by appointment) with the Courtenays to the Temple of Vesta, and the Ch. of S. Maria Cosmedin, commonly called Bocca della Verita, where is the ancient fountain into whose mouths the Romans put their hands when taking an oath, to attest its truth. Here we met with a small adventure; we found the church door locked, so waited for some time, and by and by a gendarme came up, and a man with a document of some kind in his hand, whereon the doors were unwillingly opened by an old priest, who looked very cross, and we all went in. As we were going round the church we observed some men carrying a sort of coffin or bier out of the door; we asked a boy what it was, but he did not seem to know. However when we went out, Perrini told us that a man had been drowned in the Tiber that morning and that the priest had closed the church and *refused to allow* the body to be brought in, till the Gendarme and the official order compelled him to open the door, and send out the bier to bring in the body. From hence, we went past Rienzi's house, and over the bridge to S. Cecilia in Trastevere, where is a lovely reclining statue of the saint, and many relics. This afternoon D. & I have been with Mr & Mrs Blacker, to the Villa Ludovisi, where we admired the *glorious* Head of Juno, and were much struck by the lovely view, and by the extraordinary Dove-like, weird-shaped trees, in the dense ilex-groves.

Sunday, 1 March. We went to the Farnesina, to see the cele-brated frescoes by Raffaelle and some of his pupils. Being only open two days a month, the two rooms which contain the small collection were *crowded,* more so even than the Royal Academy on a fine May afternoon, and it was amusing to study the conformation of the throat in the scores of visitors (English chiefly) who were painfully craning their necks to gaze at the roof-paintings. Then we went to the Corsini Palace, and saw the galleries, and were delighted with a few beautiful pictures among a great number of mediocrities.

In the afternoon we called on Mrs. Hartley, and did a good deal of shopping, buying little presents for England.

In the evening Major Allen called, and took us to see the art academy, where a room full of artists (or embryo-artists) were drawing from a living model, a handsome man in armour. These models have to stand absolutely motionless for two hours – sometimes more –; it must be awfully hard work. I asked the director if it was not very trying for them. 'Yes' he said 'sometimes it is, for instance, when a fly settles on their face!'

Mrs. Courtenay told me about a rather curious coincidence today. On the morning of the day after President Lincoln's assassination, when the Courtenays were away at their country-house, her daughter Florence came down to breakfast very pale and agitated and saying she had been much upset by a horrible dream she had had. She dreamt that she herself shot President Lincoln, and she described most vividly the pistol, the wound, and the expression of his face, saying she could not get the sight out of her mind, so real had it appeared.

The day passed quietly, but Florence kept recurring to her dream, and was evidently thoroughly possessed by it. In the evening Mr. Courtenay arrived from New York, with the news that the President had been shot the night before, and it was found that all the circumstances (except the personality of the assassin) exactly corresponded with Florence's dream and Florence herself was terribly agitated on hearing the news, saying she felt just as if she *had* been the murderer in reality.

Sunday, 2 March.   At church this morning, we had a most admirable sermon from the eloquent Bishop of Derry Dr. Alexander, who is really a splendid preacher. The congregation was, as usual, a crowded one, and about 200 or more stood for the Holy Communion. There were 7 clergymen besides the Bishop.

We lunched at Spillman's and then went to church again and heard the curate. After the service Mmes. Hartley and Lacy walked home with us, and paid us a long call, being regaled with Kettled rum *à L'anglaise.*

We have discovered that our nice friends, the Blackers, are Roman Catholics. We took a tender farewell of them and the Courtenays, as we leave for Naples tomorrow.

Monday, 3 March.   Mrs. Hartley came the first thing in the morning to accompany us to 'her man' − i.e. one of the numerous jewellers she patronizes, but 'her man' par excellence, because he made 8 gold bracelets for her at Xmas! She has one peculiarity of thinking all the tradespeople charge her much less than they do anyone else, out of special gallantry and devotion to her; and another of never knowing the name of a shop, though she may favour it with her custom daily. The consequence is that she could never either recommend a shop by name to us, or describe its situation, (for I don't think she knows the name of a single street in Rome, except perhaps the Corso) but must needs always accompany us to it herself and even then she often loses her way. She has various nick-names by which she distinguishes her shops in her own mind, such as 'the Scrofa shop', 'the baby-shop', 'the Christians shop', 'the Corso shop' (vague seeing the Corso has its shops by hundreds) or the shop where she bought such and such an article of jewellery. She is an odd woman, but very kind. She has never been into a boot shop, or into a mercers, or into Spillman's though she has been in Rome for months!

We left Rome at 2 o'clock and had a pleasant journey, with some very nice Italians as our companions through all that *beautiful* scenery, to Naples, where we arrived soon after 9.30, and took up our quarters in the H. de Naples.

CHAPTER III

Naples

Tuesday, 4 March. Perrini is enthusiastic about Naples, for a wonder, in spite of its being in Italy. Before breakfast this morning he came to Dearman, beaming with happiness, 'I have a surprise for you today, sir; something nice. I think you will say you have not seen anything so beautiful before.' He proposed that we should drive to San Martino, an ex-monastery from which the poor monks were driven away by Victor Emmanuel, which we accordingly did, and then his 'surprise' burst upon us, in the shape of a *most* magnificent view. S. Martino is high up above the town, so we had the whole extent of Naples just below, in all its beauty, then the glorious bay, with Capri, Ischia and Procida, and above all Vesuvius, on our left, rising grandly above the white villages and towns that cluster so dangerously near its base, the black lava fields looking in the distance like the shadows of passing clouds on the sunny plain.

After we had fully drunk in the loveliness of this glorious view, we went into the Monastery church. A perfect *bijou*, though quite small. Such exquisite marbles I think I never saw, altars, pillars, floor altar rails, all inlaid with the very finest workmanship in the rarest and most lovely marble or precious stones, agates, amethyst, lapis lazuli, and malachite appearing in lavish profusion in every corner of the church. Each of the side-chapels is rich in exquisitely painted frescoes,

Lo Scrivano pubblico

Public Scribe, Naples

La prima uscita de Sposi plebei.

Horse-drawn Carriage, Naples

splendid statues, executed with the greatest skill and delicacy, and innumerable different kinds of marble, beautifully polished, and every one has an altar inlaid with precious stones. The walls of the Sacristy are panelled with inlaid wood, of the finest workmanship, each panel representing a different subject, and all the subjects being as original and striking in design as they are bold and masterly in execution. The whole was the work of one monk, a splendid old fellow of the 15th century, who spent 43 years in executing this marvellous piece of work. His artistic skill, power of drawing and accurate knowledge of perspective, were something wonderful.

In some of the rooms of the old monastery is a most interesting museum, containing a first rate collection of lovely old Venetian glass, some exquisite specimens of medieval embroidery in silk, *and* a superb collection of Majolica, of unrivalled beauty and untold value, with which Dearman was delighted.

From San Martino we drove round by Posilipo, having lovely views all the way, and so back home.

In the afternoon we changed our rooms, moving from the ground floor to the first, and then we went to call on the Buscarlets. They live very near here, at the handsome new Scotch church. They were very pleasant, and Dearman has taken a most tremendous fancy to Mr. Buscarlet.

Wednesday, 5 March.   Hearing that there was a village quite near Naples, which had been destroyed by the lava from the last eruption, we determined to go and see it, so we took a carriage, and drove to San Sebastiano, or what remains of that ill-fated village, for the vast river of molten lava all but annihilated it and the next village, Massa di Somma. We had neither of us, till we saw this, any conception of the enormous mass of these huge lava streams; this one was half a mile broad, where we walked across it, and was composed of great rough

black-brown lumps of lava, still hot as we saw by the steam
that came forth when cold water was poured into the crevices.
It was excessively interesting to stand in the midst of this
gigantic mass, and look round on the vast desolation on all
sides, and it was thrilling to think that all this inconceivably
great tour de force of nature had been accomplished not one
year ago, the greatest that Vesuvius has know for 250 years.
Dearman had an ardent longing to see one of the craters that,
he had heard, had suddenly opened in the side of the mountain
and poured forth volumes of lava. Asking the guide if there
was such an opening near San Sebastiano, he replied that he
could shew us one, an hour's walk thence. We decided at once to
go thither, thinking it a nice unhackneyed sort of thing to do,
and rather out of the beaten track and golden visions floated
before our minds of the credit we should derive from our
discovery of the wonderful side-crater, which should hence-
forth appear in all the Baedekers and Murrays. So we left the
carriage and Perrini at San Sebastiano, fortified ourselves
against the pangs of hunger by some oranges and apples, and
started on our walk at 1.15. We found it a long tiring affair,
first over rough lava, for a long distance, decidedly hard
walking, then up and up, along a narrow path between huge
high banks – almost cliffs, and here it was *intolerably* hot. We
walked mounting always for an hour and a quarter, when we
suddenly perceived the hermitage just above us. Knowing that
this was the last point, on the way up Vesuvius, that can be
reached by carriages, we began to suspect that we had been
sold, for we didn't want to come up here at all, as we meant to
make the regular ascent of the mountain another day.
Appealing to the guide, however, we were assured that, Yes he
understood; there was a little crater that we should see, only
one 'piccolo momento' more. But our suspicions increased, and
were finally confirmed when a few minutes afterwards, we
reached the Hermitage, and unmasked the villainy of our

guide who it appears only meant that we should have a good view of the big crater! Dearman pitched into him in good sound English, which I sought to translate for the culprit's benefit, into very mild Italian, till I found all the force of vituperation was evaporating in the process. At last the happy thought struck us 'why should we not, as we *were* so near, go on up to the top then and there', and the idea was stimulated by our suddenly perceiving a party of 3 young Englishmen, riding past us on ponies, the last of whom was Prince Arthur. This seemed to prove that it was not utterly demented to begin the ascent at 3 p.m., so we set to work, sent off the crafty guide with a note to Perrini, telling him to meet us at Resina with the carriage, ordered some ponies, arranged terms with the nice guide (a government official, not a promiscuous vagabond like him of San Sebastiano) gulped down part of an omelette, as Dearman said we must have 'something to walk on' and finally mounted our little steeds at 3.10. After 20 mins. rough but not steep riding, we reached the Atrio dei Cavalli, at the foot of the mountain proper, which looked as we approached it somewhat like an Eastern encampment, with its little band of horses feeding leisurely on the scanty herbage, surrounded by swarthy picturesque ragamuffins of all ages. From this point up to the summit is a very very stiff walk of an hour or an hour and a half, all the way excessively steep, and on soft cinders, very small almost like black sand, on which one sinks in and slips back at every turn, so that the fatigue of the ascent is immensely augmented. I had 3 guides to help me; the two in front were really of some use, the one behind of none. Dearman had one, and we were, on starting, seized by about a dozen more volunteers, who descanted on the enormous difficulties of the way, which rendered at least 5 guides necessary for each person!! as well as by the 6 bearers of a *chaise à porteurs*, who almost forced me into it 'it is too far for a lady – La signora would be much better in a chair; ladies never walk all the way.' At last we shook ourselves free of these wretches, and proceeded on our way. The sun was intensely hot, and the walk was certainly tiring whilst it lasted, but it seemed soon accomplished, and then, when we – quite suddenly – reached the summit, a sight burst upon our view that would have repaid a thousandfold, ten times the toil. Right before us, shelving away from beneath our very feet, lay the deep hollow, with romantic jagged edges, in which darkly yawn the three great craters. The smoke cleared off most opportunely, as if on purpose to give us a perfect view of all the grand scene, merely curling upwards in soft filmy beauty, which added greatly to the picturesqueness of the view, and leaving clear to our eyes all the richly tinted sides of the vast hollow, bright with sulphurous hues of yellow, red and green. I had expected *thrilling interest;* for the *beauty* I was not prepared. The smoke came up beneath our feet as we walked, the ground was *burning* hot to the touch of our hands, and almost painful even through our boots, and we realized how literally we were on a volcano, when the guide pointed out to us, in several places, crevices or little apertures through which we could see the red-hot lava glowing not one foot from the surface. I pushed in a stick, and drew it out *in flames* and the guide offered to cook us eggs, which we declined, as we thought they would taste strongly of sulphur, and then he poked a bit of lava out of a hole, and gave it to Dearman to light his cigar on, which he did. We stayed up at the top about an hour intensely enjoying the glorious panorama of all the surrounding country, and the marvellous scene immediately before us, which every movement varied, according as the smoke augmented or diminished, blew on this side or on that. Sometimes the hot white sulphurous cloud swept all round and over us, but the fumes of brimstone were not so overpowering as I should have expected, though near the fire crevices the sulphur smell was tremendously powerful.

Nineteenth-century view of Naples and Vesuvius

Dancing the tarantella in front of Vesuvius

We amused ourselves by throwing stones down into the large crater, to test its depth, and there was something almost awful in hearing them go dashing down from rock to rock, echoing on the hollow loudness from those unknown depths, far down in that firey furnace which has never been seen by living man, but which has poured forth burning ruin on towns and villages, on man and beast, on fertile plains and noble trees, for thousands and thousands of years. We heard the largest stone falling for more than a minute, and then the sound ceased.

Our descent from the summit was made by an even steeper road than the ascent. I never saw anything like it. It was quite precipitous, and almost perpendicular, and looked as if no being but a fly could possibly have clambered up its steepness, and it would have been fatal to attempt to descend by it, had not the nature of the ground removed all possibility of danger, for no one could fall down, since one sinks in, 'up to one's knees,' at every step. We came down at a great pace, doing in less than 10 min. what had taken us $1\frac{1}{4}$ hours to ascend. As we remounted our ponies, and began the ride to Resina, we were charmed with the glorious after-glow that followed a splendid sunset. Then came sudden darkness, in this land of no twilight, and at 7.15 we rejoined Perrini and the carriage and reached our hotel about 8 o'clock.

Thursday, 6 March. Yesterday was a day of *such* enjoyment, such thrilling interest, that we felt we must not make this a day of sightseeing, or our minds would, as it were, be overloaded with food for thought, and we wanted a little quiet time to digest the delicious repast for soul and mind and sense, with which 'the Vesuvius' had furnished us. So the only thing, worth mentioning, we did all day, was a short visit to the inexhaustibly rich Museum here, to which we must pay many visits before we can hope to begin to know its treasures as they deserve. We strolled about in the Villa Reale, and in and out of several coral-shops, admiring many of the pretty things intensely.

Friday, 7 March.   Another day of deep interest and immense delight, second to the Vesuvius day, I almost think, but certainly second to it alone.

We left for Pompeii at 12.00, and arrived there a little before one. The lunch at the Hotel Diomède seemed much like the lunch at any prosaic wayside inn, save only a little more confused, a little more noisy, a little more American, for what it was, to have a whole trainful of hungry Yankees – with a leavening of the Old World – besieging the few bewildered dirty shock-headed handsome fellows who served as waiters, with loud calls for macaroni or wine or meat, and scrambling for seats at the table with the vigour of London gamins fighting over a handful of coppers, is what none can tell but those who have seen such manifestations of the animal in man's nature.

After lunch we went up, past the grass-grown mounds of earth thrown up in the excavation, into the City of Pompeii, and found just at the entrance, the small museum of treasures found in the ruins, though the vast majority of these are in the Museum of Naples, and this local one is only in course of formation. The most thrilling things were the casts of the bodies of 5 or 6 persons, whose precise form is preserved by the lately discovered and wonderfully ingenious method of pouring liquid plaster of Paris into the cavities, formed by the decompostion of the bodies, after their molten covering had hardened round them. In this way the exact shape is seen, and the positions of the various unfortunates when their sudden fate overtook them, faithfully indicated. The bones remain in their right places, within the plaster of Paris, and even rings on the fingers can still be discerned. There are numbers of human and animal skeletons, and we were amused by seeing the skeleton of a sucking-pig lying in the dish on which it had just been served up.

From the Museum we began our exploration of the more important of the buildings of this city of 2000 years ago. We should have required 9 days, the guide said, to see every house, but I think in the 3 hours of our walk along the streets, we saw all that was best worth seeing, and it certainly *is* worth the journey from England to see Pompeii alone. The straight streets, evenly paved with lava, worn into deep ruts by the wheels of the heavy waggons of those ancient times, with high causeways on either side, and at every cross road, stepping stones from side to side, for the convenience of foot passengers in dirty weather, the multitudes of shops, many still revealing their character by the remains of huge oil jars, corn mills, or wine amphorae, others by trade-signs, the houses delicately and tastefully decorated with frescoes as fresh and bright and soft in colouring as the day they were buried from the light of the sun. The baths, with appliances for hot, cold or tepid water, dressing rooms, and every luxury that the 19th century could devise, the temples, the forums, the Theatre, the tombs – all were interesting in the highest degree, and produced an impression such as no book, no hearsay evidence, nothing but personal experience, can give any idea of.

There was a great rush for the return train to Naples, and in the end Dearman only just managed to secure a seat, with 9 Italians, in a 2nd class carriage, while I was the 18th person in a saloon, and had there a most pleasant chat with Mr. John Fowler, C.E.,[13] just come from Egypt with Dr. Lethaby[14] and Professor Owen;[15] the latter was next but one to me.

[13] Sir John Fowler, Civil Engineer.
[14] Dr. Henry Lethaby, chemist.
[15] Sir Francis Cunliffe Owen, Director of S. Kensington Museum, assisted Sir Henry Cole in the International Exhibition in Vienna, 1873.

Saturday, 8 March.   We spent 2 hours this morning in the Museum, devoting all the time to the ancient statues, and above all, the magnificent bronzes, from Herculaneum and Pompeii. We think it so much the best place, with so large and interesting a museum, to see only one department of it at a time, and that thoroughly. The bronzes were splendid, especially the Faun from Pompeii, and the charming figure supposed to be Pan, listening to Echo, and the exquisite Head of Plato.

In the afternoon we went, by previous arrangement, with the Marquis Palmieri, a young man whose acquaintance we made at dinner yesterday, and who seems to have taken wonderfully to us, to see the Royal Palace and Park at Capo di Monte. He was very pleasant, and it was good practice in talking French, but it is slightly slow to have to make conversation for 4 hours consecutively (for he sat next to us at dinner afterwards) with a person with whom one has nothing much in common. He amused us by his *intense* politeness, and foreign ceremoniousness, escorting me with his arm all over Capo di Monte, and even up the stairs in the hotel, and afterwards in the smoking room, walking solemnly right across the room to Dearman, to shake hands with him and say goodnight. Capo di Monte has a *splendid* view, loads of modern pictures, very little porcelain, and a splendid mosaic from Pompeii; but not much else.

The park and woods are very nice. We are much entertained by a large family of Americans, whom we call the Twains, because the *pater familias* has evidently modelled himself especially in the cut of his beard, on the picture of Mark Twain on the cover of *Innocents Abroad.* (1st Ed.) The resemblance, moreover, is not confined to form and feature, face and limb, for our friend shares to the full his prototype's peculiar views on the subject of High Art, oracularly giving it as his opinion, this morning at breakfast, that 'he was sick of old masters, and for his part he thought the worst copy a fine lot better worth looking at than the best original; it fills the eye more, Sir.' He is more tolerable than his wife and daughters, however, for today when he said to his wife 'I should rather like to go to church tomorrow, just for once,' she replied, 'To church Oh! nonsense; nobody goes to church when they are abroad; the Harveys were in Europe for months and they never went, so I'm sure *we* needn't.' And his eldest fair daughter, Angelica by name, on hearing Dearman's glowing account of Vesuvius which he wound up by saying that it really did seem like the entrance to the Infernal Regions, remarked that 'She calculated she and her sisters would get to the Infernal Regions quite soon enough themselves, without going right away to the top of Vesuvius to see what it was like.'

Another daughter entertains the assembled multitude, on all possible occasions, with a loud nasal discourse, relating passages of her own history from her earliest infancy, and narrating the experiences of all her friends and relations, whom she makes out all to be 'Oh! vurr rich indeed, vurr rich, and vurr refoined you know.' *She* does not mention the fact her honester father confided to Dearman that he is a *druggist* from Cincinnati, who has made a fortune, and come out to enjoy it! He told Dearman that the American ladies have a perfect rage for tobacco, or anything to 'stimulate the nerves,' and they are now delighted with a prescription they have just hit on, for the enjoyment of 'a new sensation'; they paint the whole of the inside of the mouth, tongue, etc., with snuff!! They (the Twains) seem to bring a supply of chemicals with them for every morning at breakfast, one of the girls takes a little parcel of powder from her pocket, portions out a small share for each of the family, wraps each of these in wafer paper, and distributes them. This is quinnine 'in case of bad smells you know' – a 'case' that must arise pretty often in Naples, by the way. Dearman imitates these Yankees to such an extent, that he is positively fast acquiring the twang, and to such an alarming extent has the harmful influence already worked on him, that the editor of the Swiss Times, with whom he had some conversation the other day, went forthwith and put us in to the List of Visitors as Mr. & Mrs. J. Dearman Birchall. U.S.'

The Twain family are the very worst specimen of Yankees we have ever seen, and we now more than ever appreciate the difference between such as they are and the really better class of Americans, of which the Courtenays are a pleasant example. Mr. & Mrs. Courtenay notice and dislike the regular bad Yankee tone just as much as we do – more indeed. The Twains (Bates is their real name, by the way) have been for ages here in Naples, and yet had never once thought of ascending Vesuvius, nor of visiting S. Sebastiano, in fact we do not know of a single thing they *have* seen. What such people come to Italy for, it is difficult to perceive.

Sunday, 9 March.   We went to the handsome new English church this morning, and in coming out, met Dr. Pyemont Smith, his wife and daughter. Dearman had thought he saw them across the church, so we waited at the door for them. They were most pleasant, and we went for a stroll in the Villa Reale with them, and they asked us to join them tomorrow in a long walk to Camaldoli, which we agreed to do.

In the afternoon we went to the Scotch church, to hear Dearman's beloved Mr. Buscarlet; it is a very nice, pretty little church. Our genial old Scotch friend Mr. Sanderson welcomed us, delighted to see us 'in such a good place'. Then we walked about in the Villa, which was *crowded* and very gay and bright-looking.

Monday, 10 March.   We had a delicious long walk to the Monastery of Camaldoli, the highest point near Naples

(Vesuvius excepted), from which there is a *most superb* view, said to be the finest in Italy. The party consisted of the Smiths, an Italian lady, the Marchesa Cedronio, and her brother in law, Auralis, a *most agreeable* man, a Mrs. & Miss Homer, English, and ourselves. We left at 10.30, and were back at 5.30, having sat a long time enjoying the view (and some oranges and Marsala) at the top. It was tremendously hot – more so I think than we have ever had it, but a *splendid* day, with an enchanting sunset. The Twains have disappeared to our unfeigned delight.

Tuesday, 11 March. Although we have made an appointment with Miss Le Jeune to be photographed on Friday, we heard so glowing an account yesterday from the Marquis Palmieri of another photographer, Ferretti by name, and Dearman was moreover so charmed by some he had seen of his, that he decided to try him also, so this morning we had a long seance with him, and were taken, Dearman and I together, in cabinet size, I alone ditto, and both of us twice in cartes de visite. The jolly old man Signor Raffaello Ferretti (these Italians have such high sounding names!) seemed to take a great deal of pains, so we hope the photographs will be successful.

After lunch we went over the Royal Palace, where we saw long suites of splendid rooms, with frescoed roofs, walls hung with silk, vases of *priceless* Capo di Monte work, inlaid marble tables, and withal the most hideous common Brussels carpets.

Then we went over several churches, the Cathedral, (where we *saw* the Chapel that is the scene three times a year of the S. Januarius miracle, but were not permitted to enter its sacred precinct) Santa Chiara, etc. etc. We afterwards met the Courtenays driving in the Toledo, so we mutually stopped, exchanged warm greetings, and learned one another's whereabouts. They are at the Russie, so after dinner we paid a very pleasant call on them. They are actually going to leave Naples again on Friday! They are summoned to England sooner than they expected.

Wednesday, 12 March.   A grand debate as to our movements. We had purposed to go by the boat at 5 p.m. today across to Messina, but this morning rose cloudier than it has been since we came, the barometer was low and we heard there was a rough sea on, outside the bay. We felt that it would be awfully vexatious to be stranded at Catania or Syracuse in very cloudy weather, and unable to see Etna or anything, and yet we felt that it would be equally vexatious, if we postponed our journey, and the next day dawned bright and clear. There was much to be said on both sides, but we finally decided to wait here till next Monday; that day is much more convenient as regards the connection with the boats to Palermo. Having thus at last made up our minds, we reflected that we must finish off the sights of Naples *before* going to Sicily, instead of leaving them till our return. So we went to the Botanical Gardens, and found them in a *disgraceful* state, beds covered with weeds, paths green with mossy moisture, and a general aspect of the most profound neglect. Some of the trees, however, were splendid, very rare yuccas, agaves, in full fruit, bananas, palms, aloes, and camellia-trees covered with hundreds of splendid flowers.

After lunch we drove to Herculaneum, stopping on the way to survey the process of macaroni making. This we did very satisfactorily and thoroughly, and it was interesting and amusing, though some of the operations hardly conduce to an increased relish for macaroni on the part of the spectator. The rough meal of which it is made, is first of all carefully sifted by being passed through a succession of sieves, then poured into a large trough, and then threaded by being vigorously *stamped* on by a bare-footed dirty vagabond, then rolled hard under two large rollers, and then being of the consistency of dough, put into a huge leaded press, which is then squeezed down upon it with enormous force, by means of rough levers, in the shape of long poles, worked by about six men. At the bottom of this press is an iron plate, cut with holes of the shape of the kind of macaroni desired, through which the dough passes, and from which it comes out in long tough strings, hollow or not as the case may be. These are then hung on long sticks, and exposed to the sun to be baked, and the process is complete.

We found Herculaneum extremely interesting, much more so than we had expected, for we fancied that it had been so completely destroyed by the red-hot lava, that hardly any remains were to be seen, but though only a very small part has yet been excavated, that part is really as interesting as Pompeii, in point of quality, though not of variety and quantity. We first went through the dark subterranean remains of the amphitheatre, each carrying a candle, and then we visited the more recent excavations of several houses, much like those of Pompeii, with frescoes still bright on the walls, the statues &c. have all been removed to the Museum.

From Herculaneum we went on to La Favorite, a Royal Villa, with a large well-timbered garden, very pretty and pleasant to wander about in, with its shady winding paths. The Villa itself is nothing particular, but commands a most lovely view; one of the very most charming we have seen. The latter part of the day has been so brilliantly fine, and so much more settled-looking than the morning, that we are half – but only half – tempted to wish we had boldly gone to Sicily this evening.

Thursday, 13 March.   Today we have had a most delightful expedition to Baiae and the neighbourhood. Leaving in a carriage and pair at 10.15, we first of all drove to a shop, to lay in a small store of biscuits and things, as we did not trust the

lunch capabilities of the Baiae Trattoria. Then we went
through the long tunnel called the 'Grotto di Posillipo, nearly
a mile long, and lighted by lamps, to Pozzuoli (anc. Puteoli) a
most picturesque old town, in an exquisite situation. Here we
left the carriage, and went to Soffatara, a half extinct Volcano,
and walked at the bottom of its large crater, the ground all
sounding hollow beneath our feet, and echoing weirdly when a
stone was thrown, and puffs of smoke coming out of the hill
sides above us, among the bushes. When we reached the active
mouth of the crater we realized the force of volcanic agency
almost as much as — in a certain way even more than — we had
done on Vesuvius, for here was a sort of cavern, brilliant with
orange-coloured sulphur, pouring forth volumes of hot steam,
and roaring with tremendous loudness, and close to us, so that
we could and did actually creep within it, though the heat was
almost overpowering, and the sulphur-fumes nearly took away
our breath.

From Soffatara we walked on to the ruined amphitheatre of
Pozzuoli, a *most* interesting one, as it is wonderfully complete,
and yet absolutely untouched by the hand of the restorer, and
it shews more perfectly than we ever saw, all the mechanism of
the internal arrangements &c. of the ancient amphitheatres.

Rejoining the carriage, we drove on towards Cumae,
passing the Lake Avernus, of classic fame, and then through
the fine Arco Felice, the old Town-gate of Cumae, from the
other side of which we looked down upon the scattered ruins
that are all that remain of the ancient city. Here, turning back
to the left, we went through another long 'Grotto', a
subterranean tunnel of great antiquity, leading from Cumae to
Lake Avernus, and evidently very little patronised by visitors,
as it was carefully closed by a gate, which a man opened to us
at a charge of 9 francs! and then he and about half a dozen boys
(all requiring extra fees) preceded us with torches through the
tunnel, which is two thirds of a mile long, very low indeed,

and of course, absolutely dark. The road was excessively bad, the wheels suddenly sinking into enormous holes every moment and the roof was close above our heads as we sat in the carriage, so that of course the coachman and Perrini had to leave their seats on the box. At length we emerged on the brink of Lake Avernus, and then we drove on past the Grotto of the Sibyl, and further on the baths of Nero (where we were in a few seconds perfectly drenched with the almost boiling steam, in a little subterranean passage into which we were conducted by a small boy, naked to the waist, and looking as if all the life had been boiled out of him) to Baiae, a small village, surrounded by the ruins of temples and palaces and situated on the shores of the most lovely of bays.

Here we stopped to bait the horses for half an hour and Dearman and I sought some 'quiet nook' to eat our lunch *al fresco*. This very modest desire proved difficult of realization, for the local guide, whom we had requested to take us to some good point of view, intending there to sit and feed in peace, proceeded to lead us up to the fort! We felt keenly the absurdity of our position as we marched solemnly up to the sentinel on duty, our guide preceding us with our parcel of cakes (which kept coming undone and dropping its contents ignominiously) and our bottle of Falernian wine. The sentinel, after some parley, called the corporal; the corporal was very polite, and would have called the captain only the captain was out, so the corporal couldn't take upon himself to let us in, and we therefore retired, feeling decidedly small, though we never in the least degree expected to be admitted within the fort, and indeed did not desire it, except that we wanted some place of refuge, for we could hardly make a halt in the public street, and enjoy our lunch with the crowds of men, women and children round us, that would infallibly have gathered on the instant. We therefore marched on for some time along the high road, looking in vain for our quiet nook, till at last in despair we darted into a vineyard by the roadside, and began, standing, to discuss our biscuits. No sooner did the ancient owner of the vineyard perceive us, than, instead of turning us out as trespassers, she rushed out with two chairs, and a beaming smile of welcome! So our troubles were over.

After our frugal repast, we returned to the carriage, and drove homewards, stopping on the way to ascend Monte Nuovo, the small volcano that sprang up in one night, in the earthquake of 1538. It is only about 500 ft. high, but the ascent is rather hard-work, as the soil consists of sharp loose stones, and there are numerous lava-walls to be scrambled over. When we reached the top, we found ourselves at the brink of an enormous crater, very deep, but now quite inactive and partially grass-grown. The view all round us was most splendid, and our drive back to Naples, with the rose tints of the setting sun on Vesuvius, was a fitting close to a most charming day.

Friday, 14 March. Our new acquaintance, the Marchese Palmieri, has been most assiduous in his attentions, calling both on Tuesday and Wednesday when we were out, and paying us a visit at about ten o'clock yesterday evening.

This morning we visited the churches of the Jesù & S. Domenico, and at noon went to Miss le Jeunes', by appointment, to have our photographs taken. She is a most original person, very short and abrupt in manner, wasting no words, and ordering her clients about like children, but she gives the impression of being a true artist, and is certainly the most painstaking photographer I ever saw. She was an hour and a quarter at work on one, and only took 2 portraits, the rest of the time being spent in posing me! Her first proceeding was to pull down all my backhair, in order to fix the rest against my very skull; her second, to cover up the white lace on my dress with some little strips of black, and her third, to powder

Emily photographed by E. le Jeune, 14 March 1873

Dearman photographed by E. le Jeune, 14 March 1873

my face! She did not bestow so much time on Dearman, though he says he felt like a small child with its schoolmistress, when meekly obeying her directions. She would not allow either of us to be present whilst the other was being done, and she had no assistant whatever.

In the afternoon we paid our 2nd visit (walking) to San Martino, and after dinner went to the Buscarlets, where we spent a most pleasant evening. Dearman is as charmed as ever with Mr. B.

Saturday, 15 March. We spent five hours at the Museum, from 10 till 3 today, and it was most delightful, as we saw those parts to which we devoted this, our longest visit, very thoroughly indeed. We first went through all the sculptures we had not before seen, and were beyond measure impressed by the majestic Farnese Hercules as well as by the Farnese Bull and many other ancient statues. Then we went through the Egyptian rooms, and then through the splendid collection of ancient Etruscan vases, the largest and finest in the world. The relics from Pompeii, of course, form the chief attraction of the Museum. We had before seen the frescoes and the bronzes: today we saw the jewellery; the delicate and finely wrought gold ornaments, the exquisite cameos and intaglios, far finer than any modern skill can produce, and the superb onyx tazza called Tazzetta Farnese, with a raised head of Medusa on one side, and a relief with seven figures on the other. This, and an antique vaze of dark-blue glass, with white reliefs, were perfect gems. Then there were all kinds of Pompeian memorials, such as cloth, thread, silk, bread, walnuts, corn, beans, figs, &c. &c., the loaves of bread all perfectly retaining their shape, and one being stamped with the name of the baker. We were much interested in a beautifully made model of one of the Pompeian houses (known as the House of the Tragic Poet) *as it was,* and also in models of the Temples of Paestum.

We walked through the large and carefully arrange library, the collection of Pompeian M.S.S. on papyrus, (some still rolled up in charred black masses, others in the process of being unrolled, others again opened out, on gold-beaten skin, and clearly decipherable) and the very extensive collection of coins, but to these we did not give the same careful examination as we had done to the bronzes, frescoes and relics.

After lunch at the Cafe, we drove up behind S. Elmo, past the Villas Floridiana and Belvedere, to Posilipo and the Grotto of Sejanus. It was an enchantingly beautiful afternoon, and the views were lovely all the way. In the evening we paid a very pleasant call on the Smiths, and then had a walk in the moonlight.

Sunday, 16 March.   To church morning and afternoon, hearing the Archbishop of Dublin in the morning. Our photographs have come from Ferretti, and we are much pleased with them. As photographs, they are *perfect*. After church this afternoon, we took a stroll on the promenade, and then drove up the Posilipo, and visited Virgil's tomb, and then scrambled up some vineyards, terrace after terrace, (all the time trespassing wilfully) in the hope of getting a clear sweep of view for the sunset, which we succeeded to a great extent in doing, and it was a most splendid view. Vesuvius has been perfectly clear today, and, strange to say, hardly smoking at all. Hitherto we have always seen it smoking furiously.

Monday, 17 March.   A very busy morning, preparatory to getting off for Messina in the afternoon. Dearman was up before sunrise, and off for a second visit to the lava-fields at S. Sebastian, from which he returned at 9.30, having had a most satisfactory time, and a minute examination of all the curious phenomena there to be seen. Then he went off to the photographer's, to be taken cabinet size, and I went to the hairdressers. I had a series of woes and misfortunes, for first of all the stupid driver drove me to a stationery shop, with 'Parkins & Gotto' over the door. I asked him 'Is this 6 Str. Caterina?' and he assured me it was, so I concluded that Baedeker (on whom I was relying for the best coiffeur) was mistaken, or that the shop had changed hands since the last edition, so I told him to drive to the next mentioned place, 180 Toledo. Upon arrival, this too proved to be a stationer's shop, but I thought it would be *too* humiliating to confess to a second defeat, so I tried to look as if it was all right, descended from the carriage, paid off the intelligent cocchiere, and entered the shop. There I bought some foreign paper, and asked for the best coiffeur's. I was most politely directed to a certain Maddaloni, a quarter of a mile off, so thither I proceeded, found the place, rejoiced to perceive 'Salon pour les dames' over the door, entered and found myself in the midst of half a dozen white-sheeted gentlemen *being shaved!* I hastily asked one of the hairdressers in French for the ladies' room, whereat he looked blank, and before I had time to repeat the question in Italian, the gentleman he was shaving looked up and politely offered to act as interpreter. I soon found the outside superscription to be a snare and a delusion, inasmuch as there was no ladies' room at all, so I made my escape with all speed, took another carriage, and ordered the man to drive me home, in disgust. We had not gone far when the horse suddenly fell! I sat still, supposing he would soon pick himself up, which after a few moments he did, and then it appeared that the shaft was broken. The coachman assured me he would soon tie it up and begged me to keep my seat, but I didn't see the fun of waiting till a shaft in two pieces was made into one, so paid him his fare, and continued my journey on foot. And then, quite near our hotel, I perceived the very hairdresser's shop I had sought at first! That idiot of a driver had never taken me to the address I gave him at all, and the street had no name up, so I could not correct him when he assured me it was right. However, in the end I had my hair cut and brushed most comfortably, in a very nice 'Salon pour les Dames'. Then we did our packing, and made final arrangements as to leaving the bulk of our luggage at Naples, sending cards to the Buscarlets and the Marquis, &c., dined at 3.30 and then before five, went on board the Tiger, a very good boat apparently which is to convey us to Messina. It was a very calm afternoon, the sea as smooth as possible, but the sky cloudy, and the bay greyer than we have ever seen it.

Our fellow passengers are deeply uninteresting, and we are the only English on board – no Americans even. We had a delightful voyage, past Capri and into the open sea – Dearman and I stayed on deck till 10 o'clock by which time everyone of the other passengers seemed to have retired to rest. We have a head-wind, so I suppose it will be a slow passage. Dearman and I have succeeded in obtaining a private cabin, a very decent one too.

CHAPTER IV

Sicily

Tuesday, 18 March. The sea was extremely rough in the night, especially about 2 a.m., when we were aroused by the steward marching in to shut our window, as the waves were dashing in. Dearman and I rose and went on deck at 4.30, as we wanted to see Stromboli, and we were fully rewarded, for it was a most delicious morning, the moon shining brightly, the air delightful, especially after the heat of the cabin, and Stromboli very grand in the distance. We drew nearer and nearer the Volcano, passing it quite close at about eight; the sunrise tinting the smoke from the crater before we saw the sun above the water. Stromboli is a very fine mountain, rising with its steep pyramid form, straight up from the water. When we first saw it, we were on the crater-side of it, but we afterwards skirted the island, and saw the little town that nestles at the base of the volcano, which is so obliging as always to pour forth its lava on the other side, never touching the town. The sea was very decidedly rough and proved too much for nearly everyone, even the sailors being affected by it, and I believe all the passengers suffering more or less with the exception of myself and an old German gentleman. None of the ladies quitted their berths, till just before reaching Messina, when they emerged, pale and wretched-looking. I was on deck the whole day, from 4.30 till our arrival at 2 p.m. except when I went down for breakfast at 10, and the party at that meal consisted of the Captain, the mate, the old German, an Italian gentleman, and myself.

I enjoyed the voyage excessively, the motion was delightful, and the strong wind most delicious, though towards the end it blew a *perfect hurricane,* and we were soaked through with salt-water, even on the high summer-deck. The roughest part was, singularly enough, just as we entered the straits, and passed between Scylla and Charybdis; the whirlpool seemed very real just then, and the sand from the shore was blown in yellow clouds with the fury of the wind.

The only ones of our companions with whom we at all fraternized, were the afore-mentioned old German and two young friends of his, one a grandson of Blücher, the other a Prussian officer, and a remarkably pleasant fellow. These two youths had been very seedy early in the morning, but later in the day recovered themselves and came up on deck. The three Germans, Dearman and myself, and two other foreign gentlemen, were the only ones out of all the passengers who shewed up at all.

We reached Messina at 2 p.m. seven hours late, having had a 21 hours' passage! We have a very comfortable apartment, and met some pleasant English people at dinner.

Wednesday, 19 March.   We left Messina by the 7 a.m. train, that being the only one unless we waited till 3.30 p.m. The railway to Catania runs through splendid scenery, very like the Corniche, only more tropical looking, and I think even finer. It was an exquisite morning, and the views all the way were most enchanting. The line runs close to the sea, which was blue and sparkling in the morning sun. We reached Giardino, the station for Taormina, at 8.30, and then had a steep drive of 3 miles up the zigzags, to Taormina, the ancient Taoromenium, romantically perched on a ledge of rock 500 ft. above the sea. The first view of Etna, seen just before we reached Giardino, was extremely imposing, a huge snow-covered mass of mountains, the top then quite clear, and the smoke visible, but, during the greater part of the day, the summit was more or less veiled by clouds. There is a great deal of snow now, so much so that the mountain is inaccessible, and no-one has succeeded in reaching the top as yet this year.

We drove through the one long street of Taormina to the Hotel Timeo, at the farther end, an unpretending but very fair inn. Here we have a large, airy, and thoroughly clean apartment, at the top of the house, and with a glorious view of Etna and the sea. Unfortunately Dearman is not at all well, and has been obliged to keep very quiet all day, which is disappointing but it is a comfort to be in such a healthy place, and I hope he will soon be all right again.

We both stayed in quietly all the morning, but Perrini and I just went to the Theatre, to see the sunset about 5.30. The Theatre is a *most* interesting ruin, Greek originally, but partly remodelled by the Romans. It is excessively picturesque, being overgrown with *huge* cactuses, and hosts of wild flowers, and its situation is perfectly magnificent. I never in my life saw so beautiful a place as Taormina, and the Theatre is the best point of view, as it is on a rocky ridge which commands the coast in both directions, to the south as far as Syracuse, to the North up to the Straits of Messina, with the Calabrian mountains opposite. Southwards we saw a succession of lovely bays and fine headlands and capes, the first being the promontory on which once stood the ancient city of Naxos, the first Greek colony in Sicily, quite close to Taormina. Taormina itself is rich in the ruins of palaces and castles, Greek, Roman, Saracen, and Mediaeval. Behind the village rise precipitous cliffs, the highest of these being the citadel of Mola, a very fine rocky peak. Mountains of various forms and heights stretch all the way from the hills behind Messina, to Etna, and the near foreground is bright with fresh grass, orange and lemon groves, and these splendid cactuses, which grow to the height of trees, and the fruit of which is a favourite food with the natives. The sunset was magnificent; the clouds completely cleared off from the summit of Etna, and the sun, setting just to the right of the great mountain, tinted it with the richest warmth of light, whilst the after-glow seemed to illuminate the whole of the sky.

I dined at the *Table d'hôte,* in company with an old man who never opened his lips, and an Irish gentleman with whom we had travelled in the morning. Four English ladies were taking tea at the same time, but were very quiet and sober. Our German acquaintances of yesterday are at the other hotel here.

Thursday, 20 March.   I was energetic enough to get up at five to see the sunrise and made my way in the moonlight with Perrini to the Theatre. I found myself not the only early riser, for there I fell in with our German friends, who were most agreeable, and with the young Irishman, Mr. Grainger. The four English ladies were also there, and several others. The sunrise was splendid, even finer than the sunset of the previous evening, the sun rising from the sea, just south of Calabria, the whole eastern sky gorgeous with red and yellow and purple, and the snowy summit of Etna glowing with the red reflection. And then when the sun was fairly above the horizon, and its light spread gradually over the whole landscape, the pretty village, then grey rocks, and the green fields, and the blue sea, all woke to life and brightness.

Dearman is better today, but by no means well yet, so he is staying quietly in bed, in the hope of being able to enjoy this lovely place tomorrow.

We are reading Hans Andersen's *Improvisatore,*[16] and are charmed with the intensely vivid, and perfectly accurate, pictures it gives of Italy and the Italians.

---

[16] Subtitled *Life in Italy* published in 1845, the first of the author's books to be translated into English.

I had a capital walk this morning, up to Mola, the ancient citadel, possessed successively by Greeks, Romans, Saracens, and Normans, and almost unrivalled in natural strength, perched on its precipitous cliff, which is accessible only by one steep winding path, the same up which Dionysius of Syracuse clambered, one winter's night, four hundred years B.C. in his attempt to surprise the garrison. I started at 11.30, so I made the ascent in the very hottest part of the day, and I afterwards found that it is customary to make it only either very early in the morning, or else in the evening. I certainly found the heat something tremendous, and it is a very rough, stony path, and extremely steep, but by no means a long walk, for Mola is only 2400 ft. above the sea, and Taormina is situated 450 ft. to begin with. There is a little village clustering round the ruined castle, and here I was much struck by the clean, tidy appearance of all the natives, and by their independent bearing, so different from the whining servility of the Italian poor, who one and all invariably beg of every passing 'forestière'. Here in Mola, not one person asked me for a sou, although I had a perfect swarm of small boys round me, who all stared and smiled amiably, and that was all. Italian children are taught from their earliest years to beg, and even bright merry healthy-looking little creatures, as soon as they see a visitor, put on a woeful face, and assume a melancholy whine, as they assure you they are dying of hunger, and implore a sou to buy a little macaroni! The people of Mola seem happy, industrious, and prosperous, in their remote mountain home. The view from the Castle is very extensive, and extremely lovely, Etna to the right, the sea in front, its beautiful coast-line right and left as far as Syracuse and Messina, the mountains of Calabria a grand background to the blue water, to the left, mountains and villages bare rocks and bright vineyards, the foreground, first the picturesque Castle of Taormina, 1400 ft. high, and a thousand feet below that, the pretty village, with its ruined towers and palaces, and above all its splendid old Theatre, while behind the Citadel are, range above range, the mountains which stretch away into the brigand haunted interior of the island.

On my way down, I visited the old Castle of Taormina, and lower still, turned aside to see an old Roman reservoir, very fine, and in a quite marvellous state of preservation. My guide, the brother of our landlord, was very intelligent, and entertained me with much conversation. He speaks fair Italian, but the familiar language of the natives here, is a villainous patois, which even Perrini fails to understand. To our great gratification, we find that we have the honour of introducing our much-travelled courier to a *terra incognita*, as he has never been here before! He has touched at Messina several times, but knows nothing of the rest of Sicily and he is perfectly enraptured with Taormina. He is really *enthusiastic* about it, the first time we have seen him so about any place, and he says he never, in all his travels, saw such lovely scenery.

The party at this evening's *table d'hôte* consisted of a German doctor, (who has been here 3 months, but never goes out, sleeping all day long instead, and who is in consumption and eats *raw meat* for dinner every day, to the great horror of spectators,) and myself! but the four English ladies were at tea at the same table, and were most pleasant and lively. They are a Mrs. Woodward Scott, and her 3 daughters, and are making a most spirited sort of tour, without courier, servant or attendant of any kind. They have been travelling since last summer, and are now doing Sicily, prior to starting for Greece, Turkey, and Asia Minor! We hear much of the brigands; they are decidedly on the increase in Sicily, and the peasants are said to be in league with them. Even the immediate neighbourhood of Palermo is haunted by them, and the whole of the interior is unsafe for travellers, but this East coast is perfectly safe. Last week they stopped the diligence from Girgenti to Palermo (though it was escorted by soldiers) and took out all the *registered letters,* leaving the passengers and the ordinary letters untouched, but we hear that if they don't find enough plunder to satisfy them, they have a way of cutting off the ears of their victims, if they don't carry them off bodily.

Friday, 21 March. Dearman has been much better today, came down to lunch and dinner, and went with me to the Theatre, to see the sunset. In the morning I went with Perrini to a large deserted Dominican convent near here, which commands a splendid view on all sides, and afterwards had an hour's walk by myself, climbing a rocky hill above the theatre, where I had lovely views, and found quantities of beautiful flowers, many quite new to us. We are more charmed with Taormina every day; it is by far the loveliest place we ever saw. The weather favours us greatly; today has been perfectly magnificent, and Etna clear all day to the summit.

Saturday, 22 March. This morning I had a very exertive walk, scrambling up a small mountain, and then down again by a most precipitous descent clinging on to trees, and twigs, and prickly cactus-leaves.

We left Taormina by the 4.50 train very sorry to quit the charming little place. The four English ladies waxed quite cordial to me before our departure. Perrini is almost brokenhearted to leave his dear Monastery, where he has spent all his leisure time, and of which he thinks by day and dreams by night. It is quite a new trait in his character to be so rapturously enthusiastic. We reached Catania in the evening, and found a very small and apparently comfortable hotel.

Sunday, 23 March.   For the first time in our experience, we found neither English, French nor German service so we spent a quiet morning in the hotel, and after lunch had a charming drive through this most remarkably handsome and well-built town, up to a lovely garden, that of the Villa Juliana, where we found all kinds of rich and rare flowers and trees. Flowers grow here in gorgeous profusion, whole houses being covered with our rarest hot-house beauties, but warmer in colour than we ever see them in England. We went into the Public Gardens on our way home, and also into the Cathedral, where we found a large congregation listening attentively to the preaching of an old monk.

Monday, 24 March.   This place is as different as possible from romantic little Taormina, but is equally interesting in its way. The peasants are excessively dark in complexion, often quite mahogany coloured, and the women march along carrying tall amphorae on their heads, walking erect and firm, never needing to steady their burden with the hand.

The scenery has all a certain peculiarity caused by the volcanic character of the whole region, and quite indescribable. Everything seems, as it were, heated, the vegetation is almost feverishly luxurious, the soil is a richer brown, the flowers have a warmer hue, than one sees anywhere else. Even the carts partake of the general brilliance, being gaily painted with flowers, scenes from history, mythology or saint-lore, or from the daily life of the natives, in bright colours on a yellow ground. The trappings of the horses, too, are remarkably bright and picturesque.

We had a delightful expedition today, leaving the hotel at 9.30 a.m. We drove to Nicolosi the village, 2200 ft. on the way up Etna, from which the ascent is made to the summit. Instead of finding it a barren and desolate drive, we found the scenery all the way exceedingly pretty, the ancient lava being covered with luxuriant vegetation, olives, cactuses, orange-groves, and almond trees with their fresh bright green. But the dust on the road was not white, but always black, greyish black, so much so that Dearman irreverently likened the general aspect of things to Low Moor or Kirkstall! forgetting that in this glorious island there is no black smoke, no dark shadow between us and the clear-blue sky. We reached Nicolosi at 12.30 and there the horses baited, whilst we went up the Monti Rossi, the twin peaks which were suddenly upheaved in the great eruption of 1669. We had intended to walk up, but as it was furiously hot, and a very steep path, we thought it better, considering Dearman's health especially, to take mules. Two of these animals appeared, with men's saddles on, whereat I remonstrated, and, with some difficulty, an anti-quated side-saddle was at length procured. Then it appeared that there were no bridles, such a thing being unknown in Nicolosi, and I was discomfited to find that my 'riding' was to consist of sitting quietly on the mule's back, whilst a man led it with a rope tied to its head! I protested feebly against this ignominy, but there was no help for it; I had to submit. Dearman, however, managed to shake off his guide, and was allowed to steer his mule through the village in glorious independence, whereon the sense of my humiliation became all the more galling, as I was led along behind him. The road was very bad, very steep, and very tiring, and it was covered with deep sand all the way so that even I was fain to acknowledge that it was just as well we had the mules, for the sun high above our heads poured its fiery rays fiercely down on us. About half way up, Dearman's rejected guide suddenly made his appearance. We reminded him that he had declined his services, to which he replied that he quite understood. The other man was our guide, and he had nothing to do with us. So he walked clamly on by our side, for what could we do? We could not prevent him from taking a walk up the Monti Rossi for his own pleasure, though we felt certain he had other motives in view.

By and by the ascent became so steep that the mules kept slipping about in the loose sand, so Dearman got off, and was preparing to lead his steed when a hand came forward, and a voice said 'I'll take your mule, sir' or Italian words to that effect, so the rejected succeeded at length in making himself necessary, and so insinuating himself into our service. There is nothing like persistence.

The view from the top of the Monti Rossi was splendid, and the intensely volcanic character of everything around us gave the scene an interest altogether unique. In this strange region, everything seems to go in extremes, and to be either feverishly fertile, lavishly luxuriant, or else utterly black and barren, dead and desolate. Thus we saw before us in the vast plain, numbers of pretty white villages, surrounded by rich fresh green fields, or olive woods, or bright orange and lemon groves, and picturesque towns, on the edge of the lovely blue sea, all this so beautiful and bright, and then running down between the pretty villages, away towards the towns on the shore, the bare black lava rivers, huge and broad and gloomy, whose course we could trace so clearly from the height at which we stood above them. Below us to the right lay a whole tract of country covered with black dust, which is even more hopelessly dead-looking than the lava. To our left was the large crater that threw up the Monti Rossi, the highest point of its crust, and these are named with the most striking appropriateness, for they are par excellence 'the red mountains' – being of a rich warm colour like that of ironstone. Turning round, we beheld the snow-clad summit of Etna just above us, looking near but really six or seven hours off, and on the slopes of the mountain we counted 23 craters quite near to us. It is all on so vast a scale that it gives one a far more tremendous idea than Vesuvius, of the enormous magnitude of volcanic action.

Coming down from the Monti Rossi (after a half hour spent at the top in keen enjoyment of the view) we had an instance of 'How are the mighty fallen' for Dearman, who had marched forth in proud independence an hour and a half before, was now *led* through the town in ignominious humiliation, the despised guide leading the conquered back in triumph, so that in his deep depression Dearman came to the conculsion that 'It's of no use to dodge these fellows; if they mean to have you, *they will,* no matter *what* you do.'

On our way back from Nicolosi, we visited the rich and splendid Benedictine Monastery, second in size only to one in the world, (viz. one in Portugal) now partly turned into a barracks, and the rest of it desolate and deserted, and the lovely garden all going to ruin. It was an immensely rich foundation, and the government seized all its revenues, and turned the poor old monks (all of noble birth, who had given their all to the monastery) out into the world, with one franc a day, as compensation! This secularization of convents, so extensively practised by the Italian Government, seems to us nothing short of *robbery,* and the worst of it is that they give the nation *no* religion, in place of the one they try to uproot. The government is rapacious and extravagant, and by no means popular, for besides all these monastery confiscations, which shower gold into the Exchequer, the taxation is double what it was in the time of Bomba,[17] of blessed memory. Superstition is not yet quite dead in Italy, for we heard the other day of a poor courier in Rome, who was very ill, with inflammation of the lungs. The Dr. ordered his body to be covered with *ice.* As soon as the Dr.'s back was turned, the wife tore off all the ice, and instead covered the whole of the man's body with charms, and little pictures and images of the virgin!

---

[17] Ferdinand II, King of the Two Sicilies, 1830–59, known as King Bomba from his bombardment of Messina in 1848.

The Doctor moreover ordered brandy and beeftea to be given every hour, but this the wife refused to her husband, unless he would first confess himself to the priest, and she actually kept him nine hours without a particle of food, saying it was better his body should die, than that his soul should perish ever-lastingly! The poor man refused to confess as he did not believe in the priest's power, and on this individual assuring him that he would certainly 'go to hell' he replied, 'Well, at any rate I shall have the pleasure of meeting you there!' Still the wife refused him nourishment, and she kept all the windows open, 'to let the bad spirit out' and the end of it, of course, was that the man died.

This evening we came to Syracuse, leaving Catania immediately after the 5.30 *table d'hôte,* at 6.45. We were much amused in the train, by an eccentric Italian who seemed all on wires. I am sure he never sat in the same position 10 seconds together, during the 4 hours' journey. First of all he dined, opening out a very nice valise, and taking out and carefully unwrapping one by one about 50 small paper parcels, containing everything he could possibly want, meat, bread, butter, salt, pepper, &c. &c., and arranging everything with the greatest care on a white cloth spread beside him. He then proceeded to discuss these viands, which performance occupied about an hour and a half as he kept springing up to look out of the window (it was pitch dark), and folding up some of the parcels, and solemnly replacing them in their appointed niche; then changing his mind, unstrapping the valise again, and taking one of them out again, or slightly altering its position. The whole of the meal, even sweet cakes and oranges, was partaken of with his gloves on, so when it was all finished, each parcel carefully stored away and all the straps fastened, he proceeded to *rub* his gloves with paper, (I can *quite* believe they were somewhat greasy!) and the result, even after this operation had been performed for a long time, not satisfying him, he opened the valise again, took out a packet of gloves, and chose out a new pair, after carefully considering the question of colour. These he drew on, and then he took up a book, dashed at it and turned over its pages as if his life depended on finding a certain passage, found it, and – we thought – settled himself to read. But no, he found he could not see, so he ferreted out a candle, lighted it, read for half a minute, blew it out again, put it in his valise, rushed to the window, looked out, back to his book, candle lit again, and then again blown out, darted to the window, and pulled it up with such a jerk that the glass broke, and fell in a thousand atoms. Then he drew down the blind, resumed his seat, felt cold, put on his hat, felt cold still, put on an over-coat, – but it is impossible to give any idea of his restlessness by a mere description of what he did. He kept changing his seat the whole time, sitting first on one side and then on the other, and all his movements were so sudden and jerky as to remind one of a grass-hopper.

Like the rest of Sicily, this place is full of Germans; there are hardly any English, no Americans, a very few Italians, and the rest all Germans.

Tuesday, 25 March. We find this hotel decidedly the worst we have been in, the rooms don't seem dirty, but the whole house is close and musty, the food is very bad, (*especially* the butter!) and the service most miserable, a chambermaid who speaks nothing but the Italian patois, and doesn't even know what 'acqua calda' means, and a set of untidy waiters, who are stupid, slow and inattentive, to the last degree. The only redeeming feature is that the landlord is a remarkably gentlemanly, polite and intelligent young man, and extremely handsome, and we hear that, bad as this hotel (the Vittoria) is, it is incomparably better than the other, the Albergo del Sole. If there were only a decent hotel, Syracuse would be a most charming place to stay at. Its natural situation is *beautiful,* the pretty white modern town, on the island, jutting out in the blue water, so as to shut in its splendid harbour, and connected with the mainland by a bridge or rather series of bridges most strongly fortified, there being no less than six gates, with corresponding lines of fortification. Of course by far the larger part of the ancient city was on the mainland, but here almost all traces of it have disappeared. Ruins there are, and very interesting ones, but they are very few, considering the vast extent of the place in old times, and luxuriant groves of olives and oranges cover the greater part of the city.

This morning we had a delicious drive up to the Epipolae, the highest part of the ancient city, and visited the fort of Euryalus, which, with the great wall of Dionysius, is still to be seen, with its ramparts and watch towers and subterranean passages, and from which we had a glorious view.

We took with us a local guide, whom we have engaged to shew us the things best worth seeing, as Perrini is as new to the place as ourselves. The oranges here are the sweetest and most juicy we ever tasted; in fact all fruits and flowers seem to flourish with unusual luxuriance in this beautiful island. The Museum here is very interesting, though small and over-crowded at present.

One glorious statue, a Venus, perfectly delighted us, although the head is wanting. The Cathedral here was once a Temple of Minerva, and the old Greek pillars still remain in the church, though whitewashed over. It is excessively interesting to be in a place one has known so well all one's life (particularly in the Grecian History school books) and to see, for example, the veritable Fountain of Arethusa, as we did today.

This afternoon we took a boat, and were rowed across the harbour, and up the river Anapus, the only place in Europe where the papyrus grows naturally, and it was a delightful expedition. The river is a mere stream, very narrow and so much overgrown with weeds that two of the boatmen were several times obliged to get out and drag the boat by ropes from the banks. The vegetation was most luxuriant, magnificent papyrus-plants, 15 ft. high, with their graceful heads waving on the top of their straight smooth stem, bananas, bright yellow lilies, &c. &c., but of course the most striking feature was the papyrus. It grows in immense abundance all the way up the river. We rowed all the way up to the Fountain of Cyane, a deep pool so clear that the fishes are seen swimming about, 30 feet below, with a blue colour given to them by the water. I was ambitious to take home some papyrus by way of relics despite the guides asssurance that the pith would all shrivel up and the fine stem collapse in a few days. I was determined to try, so they gathered me two, each 12 feet long, and when we landed, though we had both Perrini and the local guide with us, a 3rd servitor must needs be engaged to carry the trophies, with which he marched in triumph before us to the hotel. Poor Dearman has found the said trophies rather a trial, I am afraid, for he has spent most of the evening planning for them, cutting one into lengths to go in with the umbrellas and at last he has given up the other as a bad job, so he has peeled off all its bark, and sliced up some of the pith, to keep as specimens. It already begins to wither, sad to say, so what will it be when we reach home?

Wednesday, 26 March.   One might buy up 'Greek coins' by the bushel here, for all the little children by the wayside offer them for sale, and they seem as plentiful as blackberries. We are somewhat sceptical about them and Dearman hurts our guide's feelings dreadfully, by throwing out suspicions as to their genuineness, for this worthy is in a small way a devoted antiquarian, and invests largely in the said coins. He has also a great facility in finding them, and this morning as we were walking along a public footpath near the Greek Theatre, our guide, who was a little in advance, suddenly 'raised a joyful cry' and picked up a little dirty copper coin, 'An ancient Greek kind, sir!' Dearman remarked 'Yes, put there on purpose this morning.' 'Indeed, sir, no; *left there from ancient times;* two thousand years old, sir.'

He shewed us this morning various interesting ruins, the Greek theatre, the Roman amphitheatre, the old church of S. Giovanni — and under it the crypt, formerly a pagan temple, then used for worship by the earliest Christians, where S. Paul is said (and with much probability of truth) to have preached during his 3 days' visit to Syracuse — the Catacombs, which are *much* larger than those of Rome or Naples, and the curious and most picturesque Latomia, the ancient quarries which were used as *prisons* and for many other purposes, and which are now overgrown with trees, or planted with lovely gardens, whilst their caverns and openings of subterranean passages are covered with maidenhair. In one of these, the Latomia del Paradiso, there is a curious grotto, very large, and cut out in the shape of an S. which is called the Ear of Dionysius, and is said to have been constructed by him to listen to the conversation of his prisoners, as its acoustic properties are such that even a whisper spoken in the Latomia, is heard distinctly at a little window far up at the top of the winding grotto.

We left Syracuse at 2.30, and reached Messina about 9.45, and the whole of the journey was made in pouring rain, a regular storm began at noon, and continued all the day and night, very high Sirocco wind, and torrents of rain.

Thursday, 27 March.   This morning dawned calm and bright and beautiful, after yesterday's storm; we hear that the sea was so rough last night that the steamer from Syracuse could not get into Messina harbour at all, but was obliged to run on for Palermo, twelve or sixteen hours further.

We had a lovely drive up among the hills above Messina this morning and enjoyed the most charming views. We went on board the Elettrico at three, but she did not start till four. She is a capital boat, and we are happy in having chanced upon the two very best of the Florio steamers for our two voyages. The company seem to us deeply uninteresting, hardly any English, and for a wonder, *no* Germans; hosts of Italians.

CHAPTER V

Southern Italy

Friday, 28 March. We had a very good passage over from Messina (though several of the passengers did manage to be ill) and reached Naples at eight this morning. We were received at our hotel with open arms, found our old room all ready for us, and our old places (next to the Marquis) at dinner were reserved for us. It feels like coming home to return here and we are renewedly charmed with lovely Naples. We seemed to have a very long day, having risen at five, and being in our hotel for breakfast at eight. We read our letters, (no trifle, as there were 30 of them), a great treat after our 11 day absolute fast, and I had my hair washed, and then we lunched at our dear Grand Cafe, and called on the Smiths (and there received an invitation from Mme. Cedronio to a small party tonight) and then had a long seance at a coral-shop, choosing various things and admiring many.

The party at the Cedronios was most amusing. Though they are veritably Marquis and Marchioness, they live upon the 3rd floor of a large house with dull stable courtyard and dirty common staircase, in a most simple suite of rooms, with apparently only one manservant, and he – we suspect – imported from the stable, with white gloves and shuffling gait. Yet it was a pleasant party, and not the least stiff, though a Duke and Duchess were there; the Smiths, several other English, two Americans, the rest Italians. Music, and a little dancing, from 9.30 till 12.

Saturday, 29 March.   A very busy morning with answering some of our legion letters, and packing and making arrangements of various kinds. Then lunch at the Cafe, and we left at 2.15 for Sorrento. Train to Castellamare, then lovely drive of 1½ hours, to Sorrento, where we put up at the Hotel Sirena, very near the Tramontana, where the Empress of Russia now is, with her son and daughter and all her suite. We had heard at Naples all sorts of stories about the intensely crowded state of Sorrento; not a room to be had for any money &c, and on arriving here, we find on the contrary, that there is no end of room in this hotel, and, we are told, in all the others, except the Tramontana, so it seems that these extravagant reports have so effectually deterred those who would otherwise have come here, that the place is actually less full than usual. This hotel is very nice, and bright and fresh, and airy, and we have from our window a glorious view of the sea, with Vesuvius full before us, in all its glory. An eruption is expected very soon (Oh! that we may see it!) as the mountain is, just now, displaying great activity. The hotels here are built on the very edge of the rock, so that from our window we look sheer down into the blue water immediately below us. We met at dinner a very pleasant Englishman, an ex-Guardsman, now living in Vienna. He gave us many hints.

Sunday, 30 March.   Finding there was an English service in the Hotel Belle Vue, a mile from this hotel, we went there this morning, and found quite a nice little church in one of the rooms, the Chaplain regularly licensed by the Bishop of Gibraltar (how extensive that prelate's diocese is!) and the service nicely conducted.

After church we had a glorious walk up on the hills and we are more and more delighted with this lovely place. We returned from our walk just in time to go to the Evening service at 4 p.m., very few there, only *one* gentleman besides

Dearman. Our acquaintance of Taormina, the Irish Ultramontane, Mr. Grainger, turned up here today.

Monday, 31 March. We have today had a most pleasant excursion to Capri, going and returning by the steamer, exploring the Blue Grotto, and calling on Dearman's old school-fellow, Edward Binyar, now an artist, living on the island, and married to a fisherman's daughter, a Capri girl! We had a long time with her before he could be found, and she was very pleasant and evidently well-meaning, but she can't speak English, so I had to carry on an Italian conversation as best I could. He seems buried alive there, and, we both fancied, looked like a man who felt he had made a grand mistake. They have two nice little children, and a house in a charming situation with lovely views.

The Blue Grotto is exquisite, fully equal to all we had heard of it. The entrance being not 3 feet high, and very narrow – a mere hole – we had to lie down flat in the bottom of the boat, whilst the boatman, with some difficulty, pushed it through the tiny opening. Then, once through, we were in a large vaulted hall, the roof and sides all a lovely sort of pearly blue, and the water simply the most exquisite colour I ever saw, a lighter blue than I expected and intensely bright and brilliant, the whole producing a fairy-like effect.

This afternoon, on our return at four, we had a charming drive to Massa, and saw the Russian Grand Duke and his sister – the Duke of Edinburgh's reported fiancée.

Tuesday, 1 April. We have today had more variety of pleasure, and seen more beautiful scenery than in all our previous travels. We left Sorrento at the early hour of 7 a.m., with a local guide, leaving Perrini to take the luggage by train to Salerno. We had a delightful walk of $2\frac{1}{4}$ hours over the hills to Scaricatoja, the descent to the latter from Conti being excessively picturesque, and the path leading zigzag down an almost perpendicular precipice of about 1500 feet. At Scaricatoja we took a boat, with four rowers, and started to go by sea to Amalfi. The sea was at first rather rough, and there was a good deal of Sirocco, but the wind dropped and the water became soon quite smooth. The scenery all the way (2½ hours) was most glorious. We were both of us delighted, and even Dearman who generally hates the sea, enjoyed this boating-trip greatly. On starting from Scaricatoja we were very near the Islands of the Sirens, barren rocks on which, doubtless, many a mariner has found his grave, whether lured there by the song of the temptress, or dashed to destruction by the fierce waves of this beautiful treacherous Mediterranean. The coast is bounded by romantic cliffs, in most places perpendicular or over-hanging, but now and then retreating a little, to allow a pretty white village to perch itself on their lower rocks, in a situation lovely in the extreme, but attainable only by sea, or by steep rugged mountain tracks. The prettiest and most important of these is Positano. The rocks all the way are of the boldest and most striking forms, towering with pinnacles, which are often crowned by a grey old Saracenic fort, or else hollowed into huge caverns and romantic grottos. Amalfi, seen from the sea, is *lovely,* perhaps the most picturesque of all the pretty Italian villages. We landed, lunched at the small but (apparently) signally well-conducted and remarkably comfortable, Hotel dei Cappuccini, and then walked up to Ravello, an old medieval city, high on the hills above Amalfi possessing ruins of interest, and lovely views. It is a city of the past, indeed, with its Byzantine churches and its stately ruined palaces, for whereas in the 12th century it had a population of 32,000, now it is tenanted only by 1500 peasants.

From Ravello we descended on the other side, to Minori, and there the carriage met us, to take us to Salerno. It is a splendid drive of 1½ hours, decidedly finer than any part of the

corniche, and we saw it at a lovely time of day, just the soft
glowing time of the afternoon. The view of Salerno, as we
approached it, was exceedingly pretty, but the town itself
though large and flourishing, does not strike us particularly by
its beauty, coming as we do from Sorrento and Amalfi.

Wednesday, 2 April. Today we went to Paestum, having
previously been informed that the road could not be
pronounced safe, but that we need take no precautions
ourselves, because we should be supplied with a guard of
soldiers by the government, who thus, gratuitously, provide
for the safety of visitors. We started in much disgust, at the
thought of having a 2nd person forced upon us, for last night a
youth named Brown, whom we had seen at the Buscarlets, and
who there never opened his lips the whole evening, coolly
came to our hotel and asked us to take him in our carriage to
Paestum next day! We could not refuse, but it was a great
nuisance, for he is a boy of the most deeply uninteresting
stamp it has ever been my lot to behold, hideously ugly, and
excessively silent and dull. We cannot make him out; he has
been travelling in Italy since December *quite alone,* which
seems most odd for a boy of that age (about 15, but looks 12),
however, the most diligent pumping on my part failed to elicit
any information. He knows how to make his way though, for
he has an extraordinary amount of coolness and is troubled by
neither pride nor timidity. I have said that we met him at the
Buscarlets; well, we afterwards discovered that he had no
previous acquaintance with them at all, nor had his father, but
the father wrote to Mr. B. to ask him to get rooms for the boy.
Thereupon, kind Mr. Buscarlet, seeing the youth lonely in a
foreign city, took compassion on him, and asked him to his
own house to stay a few days. Brown came and stayed more
than three weeks! Then the little Buscarlet boy took the
measles, and the Buscarlets really wanted Brown's room

(certainly not his company) so Mr. B. gave him a hint 'Now Mr. Brown, I think as this child has measles, the best thing you can do is to clear off at once; it would never do for *you* to catch it, you know!' But Mr. Brown refused to take the hint, and calmly replied 'Oh! thank you, I am not the least afraid; I have had the measles!' and at last they actually had to tell him to go, in so many words, but he had got three weeks' board and lodgings and pleasant society for nothing. On the same easy terms he now obtained a drive of 50 miles, and a good lunch, without offering to contribute a sou, and taking everything as his right in the most astoundingly cool manner.

Most of the people drove all the way from Salerno, but some went by train as far as Battipaglia, and here the 'military escort' was to have met us. But when we arrived there, lo and behold, the escort are being changed, the old are gone, and the new have not yet arrived. Oh! yes the road is safe, we can go certainly. But if we really wish for an escort, then we can take two gens d'armes. But, by the way, it must be in the carriage with us for they have no horses, and we must pay extra for them. Will we take them or trust ourselves unprotected? We thought it would be such an unutterable nuisance to have 2 policemen crowding us in the carriage all the long drive, that we decided rather to risk the brigands, feeling all the time that if there was danger at all, there was on that special day, for of course the brigands would know that we had no escort as well as we did. We were however unmolested; there were several other carriages of tourists on the road guarded by pickets of *bersaglieri* stationed all along its course. We seemed to be the most unprotected of any, for all the peasants we met carried weapons, and every country waggon was accompanied by soldiers driven by an armed driver. We reached Paestum at 11.30 (we had left at 8) and spent 2½ hours there, exploring the glorious ruins, the finest Greek temples in the world, Athens excepted, noble Doric buildings, in the purest style and the most *perfect* ruins I ever saw of any kind. The Temple of Neptune is especially magnificent and imposing and beautiful. Besides gazing long on the Temples from all sides, we walked along the walls of the ancient city, which built of those huge mortarless Greek stones, have stood the assaults of time as well as the Temples themselves. The crevices in these old walls are the favourite haunts of snakes; Dearman saw a large one, and lizards abound in thousands and as for the shell snails! on one single acanthus leaf I counted 78! The place seems altogether wild and weird, covered with luxuriant weeds, and inhabited only by reptiles, hawks, and buffaloes, for here we saw large herds of real live buffaloes. They are fine creatures all black, with large horns and great projecting foreheads, and eyes of a fierce wildness that give a wonderfully striking expression to the face. Most of them are literally wild, but some are domesticated, and used to draw carts like oxen.

Thursday, 3 April.   We left Salerno at 8.45 in order to see the celebrated monastery of La Cava. The valley of La Cava half an hour from Salerno, is most beautiful, surrounded by an amphitheatre of fine mountains, rich in vegetation, and just now bright with the fresh green of the young leaves. We took a very nice carriage and pair, and drove up to Corpo di Cava, the pretty clean little village on the hills, close to which is the great Convent. This is one of the two Benedictine monasteries (Monte Casino between Rome and Naples being the other) for which Mr. Gladstone specially petitioned the Italian Government, and with such success that they have escaped the general secularization. Mr. Gladstone espoused their cause on account of their great learning and high character, nearly all the monks are of noble family, and are very highly educated men. Messrs. Whalley & Newdegate[18] would doubtless see, in

---

[18] Anti-Catholics.

this incident, confirmation of the Jesuit theory with regard to the Premier!

The library at La Cava is extremely valuable, and they have there a priceless collection of old M.S.S., the Gospel of the Venerable Bede, a splendid illuminated Bible of the 8th century, numbers of bulls of the early popes, the original M.S. of the 'Imitation of Jesus Christ' &c. &c.

We went down into the crypt, and saw there great piles of bones and skulls, belonging to departed monks. Then we had the great treat of hearing the organ. It is a very large instrument, and said to be one of the finest in Europe; a young monk played it most beautifully for us.

We went on to Naples from La Cava, travelling with the Messina young Englishman and his eccentric aunt, and arriving at 2.30. Then we lunched at the Cafe, read our letters, and then took a carriage and visited the Catacombs which are immensely extensive, and the passages very wide and lofty. There are many Christian symbols among the frescoes, and we were much interested.

Then we drove to the Villa Floridiana, which we had talked of so much, and made so many unsuccessful attempts to see, for it is very difficult to get to since though it is scarcely more than a stone's throw from our hotel, the road to it is so roundabout that it is quite a long drive. We were perfectly enchanted with it, when we did at last get to it. The garden is decidedly the most beautiful and the best kept up that we have seen in Italy. Nature and Art seems to have combined to do their very utmost for the position, and views on every side, are unrivalled, and the grounds are laid out with the most consummate taste, and are bright with rare and beautiful trees and flowers. After this executive day, we reached our hotel in time for dinner, but 'the old order changeth, giving place to the new' – every familiar face has disappeared, even that of the Marquis, a new race of visitors fills the table, we are even put into a new bedroom.

Friday, 4 April.   Our last day in beautiful Naples! We are
quite melancholy at the thought, for this bright cheerful city
has grown wonderfully dear to us, in the five weeks that have
nearly elapsed since first we made its acquaintance. There is
such constant source of amusement in its odd quaint street
scenes, in its lively, dirty, inhabitants, in its life, and bustle,
and perpetual movement. In one street, near the Royal Palace,
are established a colony of 'public writers', each with his own
little table, and inkhorn and paper. They seem to have a brisk
trade, for they are largely resorted to by peasant girls, who
dictate to them the love-letters they wish to send, or by
brigandesque looking drovers, or brawny country lads. Barrel-
organs, musical boxes, and all kinds of noise-making instru-
ments on wheels rush about the streets, and when they see a
'forestiere' begin frantically playing at him. Troops of glee-
singers   shout   outside   the   windows   every   evening,
Punchinellos, Marionettes, and men with bagpipes, abound in
every street. The people are as a rule, very handsome, though
the girls lose something by not having a special costume, like
the pretty Roman one. All have their beautiful black hair
neatly plaited and tastefully arranged. Flower-selling boys and
girls pursue visitors, whether on foot or in a carriage, with
unrepellable persistance, offering gorgeous bouquets of
thousands of violets, or splendid camellias by *scores and fifties,*
for 'one franc' as they tell you in English, and they are often
willing to come down to ½ a franc, and this for magnificent
bouquets a foot and a half in diameter! The pretty dainty little
victorias, with their bright, carefully polished, brass mountings, worked all in real beautiful Repoussé work, and drawn
by capital little ponies trapped in the gayest harness, and
going at racing speed, are a quite special feature of Naples, and
they are intensely cheap, only 60 centimes for a 'course' which
may extend through the entire length of the city. To give a
franc, was to bestow a munificent *buona mano* as well.

The chief thing the Italians seem to work at, is the adornment of their carriages, for if they have a few minutes to wait, they pull out a duster, and begin diligently rubbing up the brass mountings. But they are very cruel to their good willing little horses, beating them unmercifully, and working them long after they should have received the coup de grace, caring not for old age, or sores, or broken knees, or lame legs. There is more need for a Society for the Prevention of Cruelty to Animals in Naples, than in any other place I know. Then the drivers are so reckless about knocking down people in their wild course, dashing down the crowded streets without warning cry or slackened speed. And it seems that the unfortunate pedestrians have no redress, for if one is knocked down, the driver brings an action against him for getting in his way, and the poor creature is fined!

The first night we were here, we had rooms on the ground floor, and the consequence was that we were besieged the whole of breakfast time by eager vendors of goods of all kinds, first a flower girl, then a man with sticks, then a fruit seller, then a match-boy, then a man with cheap coral and lava ornaments, and scores more, all thrusting their wares and half their bodies right into the room, and discoursing volubly in Italian and (all of them) a little *English,* on the superior nature of the article they forced upon our notice. The Neapolitans are, I believe, the merriest, the dirtiest, the good temperedest, the laziest, the handsomest, the lyingest, and withal the happiest – in a careless, easy going, jolly sort of fashion, – of any people in the world. They are very abstemious in the way of food and drink, and very unambitious, so that so long as they can have a little macaroni every day, their bliss is complete, and they won't do a stroke of work more than is necessary to get just that small quantity of macaroni; they like to lie basking in the sun, and smoking, or humming a tune, all the day long. Perrini, remarking on the frequent delays we experience in getting our letters from the post, explained that 'you see poor things they have such hard work; when the letters come they first smoke a little, then they take out a letter, then they want rest, so they sit still for five minutes, then they take out another letter, and then they must smoke quietly for a while, for fear of catching an inflammation if they work too hard.'

We are amused to see the great numbers of cows and goats (the milk of both is used, but chiefly that of the latter) that are brought into the city morning and evening, and taken round the streets, to supply at each house the milk required. The oxen here are 'splendid beasts' (à la Florrie's description of her first visit to the Zoological Gardens 'the elephants are noble beasts; the giraffes are very elegant beasts, but I liked monkeys best').

On this one last day in Naples, we drove to Baiae and back in the morning, stopping only at the Temple of Serapis, which we had not seen on our former visit, and which is interesting as shewing in a curious way the alterations of level in land and sea that have taken place within comparatively recent times. The pillars of the old temple are perforated with round holes, caused by shell-fish which ate into the marble, up to a height of 20 feet, confirming the historic records that the sea covered this part of the coast to that extent, and then again retreated, some centuries ago. Even now the sea-water stands round each pillar in a sort of pool, covering its base. This temple is at Pozzuoli.

After lunch we did some shopping, and then paid farewell calls, first on the Marchesa Cedronio, who was most pleasant and cordial, and then on the Buscarlets. To them I was in the act of recounting Brown's adventures at Paestum, and we were all discussing his coolness and scrupulous regard for the welfare of No. 1, when the door opened – speak of an angel &c. and *Brown* entered, marched up to us and shook hands with all four, without opening his lips. We were all so taken aback at his apparition just at that moment, that we had great difficulty in preserving our gravity. He had come to pack up his things (which he had left at the Buscarlets,) prior to departing for Malta, the news of which departure we all hailed with joy.

Saturday, 5 April.   Being anxious to see Caserta, on our way to Rome, Dearman and I left Naples at 9.35, leaving Perrini and the luggage to come on 3 hours later. We were charmed with Caserta; the grounds are very extensive and extremely beautiful, cascades, arbours, grottos, lakelets, straight clipt high hedges, like those at Bramham, and beautiful natural woods, undulating grass-lawns, winding paths, and lovely flowers. The palace is by far the finest we have seen, being built and furnished in a style of lavish gorgeousness, combined with good taste and real appreciation of art, thoroughly characteristic of its Bourbon founders and inhabitants, and by no means to the taste of Victor Emmanuel. The grand staircase, all of the richest marbles, is one of the finest things I ever saw. Canova's lions stand on its lowest step, and the niches in the marble walls are occupied by splendid statues. The whole of the Royal apartments is princely in every detail, and even in the theatre, the place of shams par excellence, the pillars are of old African marble, and stood once in the temple of Serapis, round the altar of sacrifice.

We left Caserta at 1.45, and the long train was so crowded, that we could find room only in a smoking carriage, with our Viennese friend, Capt. Morragh, two other young English-men, very pleasant, an old English sea-captain, and an Italian. In the middle of the journey, some wretched boys threw a stone, which shivered our window to atoms, and dashed into our midst, giving me a sharp blow on the knee, which, together with the tremendous crash of broken glass, con-siderably astonished me. At the station of Segni we observed that all the officials were armed with muskets, and an old gentleman who got out there and entered his carriage, was escorted by mounted soldiers, for all the inhabitants here are on the alert, since it was between this place and Velletri that the brigands last week attacked the mail-cart in open daylight! Perrini heard an amusing story of Palermo brigandage, when we were in Sicily. The band, in great force, attacked the train from Lercara, bound the guard, shot the engine-driver dead, and began to rifle the carriages. The stoker who had been asleep, and somehow escaped the observation of the brigands, woke up, perceived the state of affairs, and while the band were engaged in their work of plunder, he turned on the steam, and ran the train, brigands and all, right into Palermo, so the robbers were taken in their own net.

We hear that Manza, the great brigand chief of Paestum and the neighbourhood, is a general favourite among the country-people, for he is a sort of Robin Hood, robbing the rich, and giving generously to the poor. He was taken prisoner once lately but succeeded in winning over his gaoler, whom he persuaded to join the band, the two eloped together, and the great robber is still at large, and seems likely long to be so.

Chapter VI

Rome

Sunday, 6 April.   In Rome once more! This morning we went at 9.30 to S. Peter's, and there witnessed the ceremony of blessing the Palms, which was performed by the Cardinal Borromeo, and the grand procession of all the dignitaries, clergy, and acolytes, round the church, out at a side-door, then, after antiphonal singing, the choir, inside, answered by the procession without, re-entering by the great doors, and back up the church. The singing was *most* lovely; we both enjoyed it greatly. There were a great many people in the church, and standing close to us, in the crowd, to watch the procession, were the Prince and Princess Louis of Hesse, attended by Monsignor Howard, a very fine-looking handsome dignitary, clad in flowing purple. He is of the Arundel family, and was formerly an officer in the English army. The Prince and Princess are staying in the same hotel as we are, the H. d'Allemagne; they travel as the Count & Countess Staufenburg, and seem to be very quiet, and to receive no more special notice or attention than anybody else.

From S. Peter's we went to our own church, which was as full as ever, and walked home afterwards with Mrs. Hartley and her nephew Capt. Hoole. In the afternoon we went to the other church, a small one, and Low, (though ours is not specially High at all) and it was *stifling* hot, and we had a long sermon from a missionary. Then we called on the Smiths, and in the evening Capt. Hoole called on us.

Monday, 7 April. We have very nice rooms, a capital salon and good bedroom, high and clean and airy, on the 3rd floor. This hotel is thoroughly clean, and the situation is considered healthy, but the *table d'hôte* is very poor. Today Dearman has one of his bad headaches (the first he has had since our marriage) and it is a very violent one too. So he is keeping very quiet, in the hope that it will soon wear itself out, and we have done nothing particular today. Besides, the day has been cold and gloomy and showery, a great contrast to the weather we had in Naples. I called on Mrs. Hartley and the Smiths. The latter are in the H. d'Italie, where also are the Matthew Arnolds, and John Grainger, whom I saw today there.

Tuesday, 8 April. We spent the morning most delightfully at the Capitoline Museum and were of course enchanted with the glorious Dying Gladiator — so familiar to us already in copy and photograph, but so far superior to all — the Faun of Praxiteles, joyous and careless, as it is so well described in Transformation — the Antinous — beautiful as befits the recognized type of manly beauty — the Mosaic of the Doves, the lovely Venus, and the child with the dove.

Here we met the Smiths, and several of our Sicilian acquaintances, (who all seem to be turning up in Rome) notably Mr. Warburg's countrymen, with whom we had made friends on the passage from Messina to Naples.

This afternoon we visited the Villa Albani — a perfect museum of ancient statues, and a thoroughly *Roman* countryhouse, with stiff, flat and yet, in its own way, pretty and interesting, garden. Afterwards we went to the Villa Medici, behind the Académie française. We had the three Pyemont Smiths, Mrs. Hartley and Capt. Hoole to dinner in our salon this evening, and spent a very pleasant evening. They, none of them, left till after eleven. We had made praiseworthy attempts to make up our number to eight, having tried, successively, to get Major Allen, the Blackers, (who, we found have left Rome) Captain Morragh, and John Grainger, but all in vain.

Wednesday, 9 April. Fortunately we were up earlier than usual this morning, for at nine appeared Mr. Warburg, just arrived by night train from Florence, and very pleasant, and soon after him Capt. Hoole also arrived, to accompany us on a round of studio-visiting. We saw the studios of the negress, Miss Edmonia Lewis,[19] of Guglielini of Lombardi (a lovely Ruth, and a charming Susanna) of Warrington Wood, (a lady in riding-habit, and a pretty Jewish Captive maid) of Mr. Ball, of Prinzi (huge ecclesiastical sculptures) of Rogers (great works for America, and mostly for public buildings) and those of the painters Terry and Strutt, the former figures, the latter watercolour sketches. Mr. Strutt's abode is at the top of a dark staircase, leading up from a dirty little stable-yard, and having 134 steps.

At four we went with Capt. Hoole to S. Peter's, to hear the Miserere, but after all it was not performed, though we did hear some singing so exquisitely beautiful and pathetic, especially a treble solo, that for a long time we laboured under the delusion that it *was* the Miserere. It was however only a part of the Long Lamentations; we heard the whole of the Tenebrae,[20] seeing all the 21 candles one by one extinguished, save one, which was hidden under the altar, and afterwards brought back, in answer, it is supposed to the prayers of the faithful.

The whole of this long service being performed in the small chapel of the Choir, the crowd was something tremendous, and the heat, perfectly stifling, and we stood there for three

---

[19] She was an American Sculptor.
[20] Tenebrae, Matins and Lauds for the last three days of Holy week.

hours. After it was all over, certain precious relics were shewn to the people from a balcony in the nave, these being a piece of the True Cross, a Thorn from the Crown, a portion of the Spear which pierced Christ's side, and the impression of His Face on S. Veronica's handkerchief. We find it quite impossible to obtain information of what is going to be done, as some of the Holy Week ceremonies seem to be omitted, and others performed, quite arbitrarily.

Thursday, 10 April. This morning we visited with the Smiths, the catacombs of S. Calixtus, and found them very curious and interesting, with the Christian symbols on the frescoes, the greatest favourites being the good Shepherd, the Fish, the Miracle of the Loaves, and Moses striking the Rock. Wandering among those endless dark narrow passages, one can easily believe the terrible stories one has heard of hapless beings, chance visitors like ourselves, straying helplessly in those weird labyrinths till death put an end to their wanderings in that city of the dead, and one's only marvel is that the guide can find his way, without any apparent assistance from clue of thread, chalked way, marks, or any such thing. From this great Catacomb, we went on to the Roman Tower, so conspicuous in almost all sketches of the Campagna, the Tomb of Cecilia Metella. Torrents of rain were deluging the earth all the morning (with short intervals) – the remains of a tremendous storm of thunder, lightning, and rain that had raged in the night. So heavy was it, that the water stood a foot deep in many parts of the road we drove along, notably near the arch of Constantine, and yet next morning all was dry and clean again!

The weather cleared at noon, and in the afternoon we went to the Pantheon, &c. and Mr. Warburg dined with us in the evening.

Friday, 11 April.   This being Good Friday, we had a quiet Sunday-like day, going to our English church in the morning, and in the afternoon to S. Peter's in the hope of at last hearing the Miserere sung to Allegri's music. In this, we were again disappointed, but we had, nevertheless, a rare treat, for we heard the most enchanting singing – and to Allegri's music – that I think I ever heard; really something quite heavenly in its loveliness. At the Sala Dante, whither we went in the evening to a grand performance of the Stabat Mater and the Miserere (but *not* Allegri's, as we found to our disgust) we heard something very different, 100 voices singing their loudest in a crowded little hall, full of English. Capt. Hoole was with us.

Saturday, 12 April.   This morning was spent in doing a certain amount of necessary shopping, in having our photographs taken for cameos, in visiting Sanlini's *lovely* cameo collection, and in doing some more studios, Miss Hosmer's (splendid tinted Medusa), Story's (glorious Medea), Poinzdestra's (very fine oil-paintings) and Zieleke's (Taormina sketch, for which we gave him a commission).

Then we went to the Barberini Palace, and saw the far-famed Beatrice Cenci, and then dined with the Smiths at the Italie. I renewed my acquaintance with the Arnolds, and they were *most* pleasant. Their two little girls, and Dick the only remaining son, are with them. Mr. Warburg was with us all the evening, and was very pleasant and entertaining. At ten I went with the Smiths to the Colosseum, to see it once more by moonlight, and we went to the very top, whence the effect of beauty and vastness was far more striking than below. Meantime Dearman, 'having had enough of mooning in the Colosseum' was taking a stroll with Mr. Warburg. He, (Dearman) was so charmed this evening with the Hotel d'Italie, that he atually engaged rooms on the spot, for us on Monday! We do not care for the Allemagne. Our rooms are beautiful, and it is a very clean hotel, but the dinner is poor, the dining-room wretched, and the guests common.

Sunday, 13 April.   At nine this morning we went off to S. Peter's and heard there a very fine musical mass, with splendid singing. There was an immense number of people, and a cardinal celebrated Mass at the altar in the East window, at the end of the nave. We were obliged to come away before it was over, to go to our own church, and there we had a most beautiful service, choral, with a large congregation, – 400 of whom, Dearman computes, stayed for the Communion. The decorations of the church were *exquisite;* anything more lovely than those of the altar and pulpit I certainly never saw.

After lunch we had a call from Mr. Warburg, and then we went to church, and after service had a delightful drive of two hours in a beautiful 'private' carriage, taking Mrs. Hartley and Capt. Hoole with us, to see the gay world turned out in full Easter brilliance, in the Borghese Gardens, and on the Pinician Hill. We dined at the *Table d'hôte*, and liked it less than ever, it was so noisy and disorderly, and the people *so* common, with the exception of a charming widow-lady, Mrs. Honywood, and the Dunlop Stewarts, a very nice-looking young couple, whom we had met in Naples. We don't feel the least regret in leaving this hotel, excepting on account of its convenient situation. (NB. the proximity of Spillman's is not undesirable.)

Monday, 14 April.   A glorious day, and *very* hot.

This morning we packed our things, and moved our quarters, and then went up the tower of the Capitol, and were perfectly delighted with the superb panorama of beautiful Rome, the whole grand city spread out around us, surrounded by its lovely Campagna, and with the exquisite mountains in the background.

Mr. Warburg lunched with us, and then he accompanied us in a *most enchanting* four hours' drive, to the Villa Mellini, on the Monte Mario, and then to the Doria Pamfili (our 2nd visit) and round through the lovely park there, now all brilliant with the tender fresh green of spring, and glowing with sunlight.

Tuesday, 15 April.   We sat in the drawingroom for some time yesterday evening, and saw Mr. Warburg perform some wonderful card-tricks, and sleight of hand feats.

There are some very pleasant people here. Today we have been to the Doria Palace, and seen there many dull pictures and some gems, especially two fine Claude Lorrains, a beautiful Joseph by Guercino, and a lovely little marble group of three little boys playing together. We have done some shopping, have received a long call from Captain Hoole, and then this afternoon we have been to the Vatican Museum. We have seen most of the sculptures, but they are so intensely glorious that we must visit them at least once more. We were almost overwhelmed with the number and beauty of these glorious statues, *all* good, not one poor thing in the whole vast collection. Those which most of all delighted us were the Head of Jupiter from Otricoli, the Laocoön, the Mercury, the Apollo Belvedere, and the wonderfully clever statues of all kinds of animals. We sat between the Arnolds and the Smiths at dinner, which was very pleasant. Mr. Warburg spent most of the evening with us, up in our salon. He leaves tomorrow morning for England.

This hot weather seems really to have set in, but it is not yet oppressive, only very delicious, and Rome is looking its very best. How we shall feel leaving the dear old place!

Wednesday, 16 April.   A most delightful day, both as regards the beauty of the weather, and our enjoyment of our sight seeing. We went first to the Borghese Gallery, and were

delighted with this finest of private collections. The pictures
which most struck us, I think, were Albani's pretty Four
Seasons (asssociated in our minds with the Improvisatore)
Titian's Sacred and Profane Love, Raffaelle's Portrait of Caesar
Borgia, his Entombment (except that the bearers seemed
almost too painfully sensible of the weight of their burden,
from the winding-sheet being so very small), Francia's S.
Stephen, (in a rich red cloak) Correggio's Dance,
Domenichino's Cumaean Sybil, Guido Reni's S. Joseph, and
some charming little Dutch and Flemish pictures.

From the Borghese we went to the Temple of Vesta, the
arch of Janus, and the Cloaca Maxima, or all that is to be seen
of it during its course. We had seen its influx to the Tiber from
the Ponte Rotto. Then we went on to the Baths of Caracalla,
and wandered about the vast ruin – the largest in Rome except
the Colosseum – with the greatest interest. It was here that
those greatest treasures of the Naples Museum, the Farnese
Bull, the Flora, and the Hercules, were found, also the
immense mosaic (of 28 pugilists) now in the Museum of the
Lateran. The excavations now being actively prosecuted, are
daily bringing to light objects of value and interest. The ruins
are most picturesque in form, and the brick work is beautifully
preserved.

This afternoon we did some shopping etc., and had a long
call from Mabel Smith. Then, in the evening, we went at
nine, Capt. Hoole calling to go with us, to a large Theatrical
party at Mrs. MacLean's, the consul's wife. There were at
least 100 English people of the best class there, and we had a
very pleasant evening. The acting all went off very well
indeed, and was exceedingly amusing. The plays performed
were 1) Popping the Question, 2) A most unwarrantable intru-
sion, 3) Turn him out. The second little farce with two actors,
was very well done by Mr. Edis and Mr. Inglis. To the former
I was introduced, and we talked for some time; I was also

introduced to Miss Haig and I talked to Capt. Hoole and to our little midshipman-friend (Messina).

Thursday, 17 April. I discovered last night that the youth we have met so repeatedly, from Nice onwards, and whose 'native county is Banff' is a certain Sir Robert Abercrombie, and is in delicate health. He was at the MacLeans and so were numbers of people, whose faces I knew, but not their names.

Today we have been to Tivoli, with Mrs. Hartley and Capt. Hoole. We enjoyed it immensely, though we had not a very favourable day, for though we had some lovely gleams of sunshine, the day as a whole was unusually grey, and we even had some slight showers. Indeed in Rome they had some really heavy rain. We found our time far too short to do full justice to the enchanting beauties of Tivoli; it would be charming to spend several days there. It is rather a long drive from Rome (20 miles each way) for just a day's excusion. We left at 2.30 punctually, and were not home till after 7.30 p.m. We went first to Hadrian's Villa, and were delighted with the pretty ruins, so extremely picturesque, and, of enormous extent. Then on to Tivoli, where we lunched in the old Temple of Sibylla, on the brink of the splendid gorge of the Cascades, and afterwards visited the beautiful falls, and the charming Villa D'Este. We had no dust coming home owing to the showers. We had been well-nigh choked on the way to Tivoli.

We dined this evening at Mrs. Hartley's, just six, the only stranger being an Italico Englishman.

Friday, 18 April. We have had a most executive day, and have enjoyed everything thoroughly. We first of all went to the Vatican for another hour at the glorious statues from 10–11, then to the Capitol, to see the Picture-gallery, and the Wolf. This last seems hedged with a sort of divinity which makes it excessively difficult of access and we feel quite proud of having

at length succeeded in penetrating to the sanctum sanctorum;
for many people leave Rome without ever seeing the Wolf at
all. For some unexplained reason, the room where it is (in the
same room is a splendid head of Brutus) and three others, are
locked up, and there is an absurd and incomprehensible
amount of mystery about it, and of difficulty in, first
ascertaining where it really is, and then of obtaining the order
to see it. We were passed on from official to official, bureau to
bureau, till we were finally ushered into a private room, where
were some of the Municipal chiefs, great swells, who were
intensely polite, wrote us out the order, signed and sealed it,
all with a solemn formality and fussy red-tape-ism that was
very amusing. It was thrilling to see *the* Capitoline Wolf, with
all its historical associations, and with the very rift, in its leg
of solid bronze, that was made by the lightning at the moment
of the death of Caesar.

Of the Capitoline pictures, the ones which most interested
us were a *very* fine John the Baptist, by Guercino, Romulus
and Remus by Rubens, and some first rate portraits by Van
Dyck.

Mrs. Hartley, Mrs. Lacy, and Capt. Hoole have gone off to
Naples today, so we went to bid goodbye, and found them just
in the agonies of getting off, at least Mrs. Hartley was in a
state of general flurry, not half ready, and in a great
excitement, Mrs. Lacy being calmly engaged on her lunch,
bonnet on, and bag in hand, and the Captain cool, cheerful
and conversational as is his wont.

From their house we went to the Farnese palace, now the
residence of the ex-King of Naples, and once the home of the
great Farnese sculptures, before old Bomba removed them to
Naples, and thereby lost them, poor man. This palace was
chiefly built of materials taken from the Colosseum (O
Vandalism) and contains some admirable frescoes by Annibale
Caracci.

After lunch we went to the Vatican, and spent three hours in the Sistine Chapel, the Stanze of Raffaelle, and part of the Picture gallery. Such a treat I certainly never had before, except in the Sculpture Museum of the same grand old palace.

The frescoes *all over* the Sistine chapel are most interesting; but Michaelangelo's enormous Last Judgement certainly does *not* give *me* so much pleasure as Raffaelle's Transfiguration, or other pictures I have seen. The Stanze are a great treat; the Loggie we have not seen properly as yet. After five, (when the Vatican closes) we called on Mrs. Gason, and did some shopping, &c. being out till after 6.30.

Saturday, 19 April. We have had quite a blow to our feelings, and the first real disappointment and sorrow of our tour – nothing less than parting with our excellent Perrini. He received a telegram last night to say that his wife was very ill, and he must return at once, so of course we set him at liberty, though with the deepest regret, for we shall miss him terribly; he is such a capital fellow in every way, and we have both grown so fond of him in the three months he has been with us. He has gone tonight, and will travel straight to London. In his place we have engaged an old fogy whom he recommended as a good courier: I hope he may prove decent, but he is sure to be a sad falling off from Perrini.

This morning we drove first to the Museum of the Lateran, and were there much interested in the inscriptions from the Catacombs, (the Good Shepherd, the Miracle of the Loaves, the Striking of the Rock, the Creation, Daniel in the Lions' Den, &c. are favourite subjects, and the Fish is a frequent symbol, since ιχθυς = Ιησους Χριστος Θεου Νιος Σωτης = Jesus Christ the Saviour, Son of God. Baptism, the Communion, and the Resurrection are frequently symbolized. We also saw through the Picture gallery and the Sculpture Museum, which contains a splendid Statue of Sophocles.

From the Lateran we went to S. Clemente, and were greatly interested in the three churches, one above the other, the lowest originally a pagan temple, and now far below the ground, with ancient frescoes and columns. We went up to the top of the Colosseum this splendid morning, and the view was most lovely, everything so bright and fresh and smiling. We also went to the Baths of Titus, and the Golden Palace of Nero, underneath them. These ruins are extremely interesting, and beautiful frescoes are still clear on the roofs, though 1600 years old; they are so excessively fine and delicate that the only ones in Rome at all to compare with them are those in the Via Latina tombs, and they were unequalled till the discovery of those at Pompeii. It was these frescoes that gave Raffaelle his ideas for the Loggie.

This afternoon we have been up the Capitol tower again, have visited one or two studios, and have driven, with the Smiths, to the lovely Villa Wolkonsky.

Sunday, 20 April. We had a violent storm of thunder and lightning, and tremendous hail, this morning, which considerably thinned the congregation. Before church, Dearman accompanied Mr. Arnold to the Museo Kircheriano (gentlemen only) where they saw some very interesting things, amongst them the very earliest representation of the crucifixion, a man with an ass's head, extended on a cross, a figure bending before it in an attitude of adoration, and beneath, in rude Greek letters, the inscription 'Alaxomenos worships his God'; this caricature was roughly scratched by a common soldier in the Guard-house of the Palace of the Caesars.

This afternoon we visited the Jesù, S. Maria della Pace [Sibyls] and S. Maria in Trastevere (Mosaics).

Monday, 21 April. This morning we went to the Vatican immediately after breakfast, and spent an hour among the

Sculptures, chiefly in the Braccio Nuova, where is a splendid colossal figure of the Nile, with little children playing round it.

From the Vatican we went to the churches of the Jesù & S. Maria della Pace again, and then to the Colonna Gallery, where we much admired some fine landscapes by Orizzonte, and the Colonna portraits by Van Dyck, and one by Sustermanns.

Then we visited the Academy of S. Luke, where are some lovely landscapes by Jos. Vernet; a fine Claude Lorrain, Titian's Vanity, a fresco of a boy, Raffaelle, and a good Susanna, by Paola Veronese – then we went into the Capitoline Museum, to see again those glorious statues, and then in the afternoon we spent three hours at the Vatican, for our second visit to the Picture gallery, Stanze, Loggie and Sistine Chapel. Of course we gave special attention to each individual picture in *this* gallery, for there are not 50 altogether, and each one is in its way a masterpiece. Guercino's John the Baptist and his S. Thomas are splendid. Raffaelle's Predella of the Annunciation, Adoration of the Magi, and Presentation in the Temple, Fra Angelico's S. Nicolas de Bari, Murillo's Adoration of the Shepherds, and his Return of the Prodigal, Guercino's S. Margaret, a fine Madonna and Saints, by Perngino, Sassoferrato's finest Madonna, a lovely Annunication, by Baroccio, and of course, the three gems, Raffaelle's Transfiguration, his Madonna di Foligno, and Domenichino's Master-piece, the Communion of S. Jerome. Then we went up to S. Onofrio, the scene of much of Tasso's life, where the oak-tree under which he sat, and other momentos are shewn to relic-loving tourists.

The evening was occupied with the illumination of the Colosseum, the Arches of Titus and Constantine, the Palace of the Caesars, the Forum, and the Capitol, by coloured flames, alternately red, green and purple, and the electric light, and it was *exquisite,* all so tastefully managed; the Colosseum lit up in this strange weird style, had a beauty indescribable and unique, without anything approaching to tawdriness. The red flames gave it precisely the appearance of being on fire. All this grand illumination took place in celebration of the anniversary of the founding of Rome, the crowds of people were immense, I had no idea Rome would, so literally, turn out in her tens of thousands. The whole way to the Colosseum was one mass of human beings, hundreds more had posted themselves on the ruined Basilica of Constantine etc, and when we reached the Colosseum, we found it so densely thronged, that we were reminded of its palmy days, when 90,000 spectators found seats in the vast amphitheatre. The crowd was all as immaculately well-behaved as possible. We saw no rudeness, no vulgarity, no discourtesy, all was refined, quiet and polite, though all the roughs of Rome were free to range among the crowd. Rome certainly is the very cleanest, quietest and best-conducted city we know, not excepting any in 'favoured England'. We are more than impressed with this fact.

Tuesday, 22 April.   A *most* interesting morning at the Vatican, exploring parts of it to which we had not before been able to penetrate. Today we procured an order for these at the door, and we found the additional pass-port of a *franc* occasionally necessary, but always effectual. We went first to the Etruscan Museum, and found it delightful; the fine gold work (now so cleverly imitated by Castellani) most lovely, and repousse work on shields, &c., also splendid Etruscan vases, a fine Bronze war-chariot, and numbers of other curious and beautiful antiquities.

The Vatican Library is excessively interesting, far from being a musty dark place, lined with shelves of dull-looking books, it is a series of large and richly decorated halls, bright and airy, adorned with gorgeous Royal presents to the Popes, e.g. china from Napoleon I, and a splendid Malachite vase from the usual quarter – (the Emperor of Russia seems to scatter his malachite broadcast from S. Paul's church Rome, to the Ballroom at Chatsworth). But other treasures in the Vatican Library are yet more interesting. In one case we saw a superb collection of *Greek* gold-designs between 2 plates of glass, which formed the bases of bottles and jugs &c, and, from their great solidity, have remained intact while the remaining, and thinner, parts of the glass vessels have decayed away. These designs are early Christian, of the 1st and 2nd centuries, and represent Peter and Paul and the other apostles, the Good Shepherd, and various Christian symbols. Other cases contained beautiful carvings in ivory, rich illuminated missals, &c.

On leaving the Vatican (after one more glance round the Sculpture Gallery) we looked in at glorious S. Peter's, 'to say Goodbye' – a most pathetic thought to us – and then, went to see the Moses, Michelangelo's great statue, in S. Pietro in Vincoli.

In the afternoon we went to the races, and saw all the beau monde of Rome there, the King, the Princess Margharita and her ugly surly husband, our Princess Alice – so bright and bonny – and Prince Louis of Hesse and the Duke of Edinburgh, who has grown extremely like the Prince of Wales. Among the crowd, we were saluted by our friend the young Marquis Palamieri who was most cordial; he came in to our carriage, and then dined with us at our *table d'hôte*, and was very pleasant all the evening. The races, as races, were a very mild affair.

Wednesday, 23 April.   We have tried the old courier whom Perrini recommended, for two days, and we don't like him at all, he is so dense and stupid, so utterly 'feckless' – so we have given him his congé, and failing in our efforts to find another, we decide to pursue our journey without one.

Today has been spent in final arrangements, and our hearts are heavy as we make them for we are grieved indeed to leave our beloved Rome. Everyone is moving off this week. The Smiths went on Tuesday, the Matthew Arnolds this morning. The latter are delightful people, and it has been a great pleasure to us both to meet them.

Tonight we go to Terni, arriving there at 12.30 a.m. in order to see the Falls in the morning before going on to Florence.

Thursday, 24 April.   We drove this morning to the Falls, and were delighted with them, far more than we had expected to be, much though we had always heard of them. They are wonderfully picturesque, and being very full of water, we saw them to great advantage, and in the vast clouds of spray, we saw a splendid rainbow, perfect in form, and brilliant in colour. The country around is charming and altogether we think Terni would be a delicious place to stay at.

We went on by the noon train to Florence, and there put up at our old Hotel, the H. de la Ville. The Smiths called at 10, just as I was returning to rest with one of Dearman's pet mustard plasters on (the *stinging* ones) so I did not see them.

Florence is extremely full — crowded —.

The Forum, Rome, by Hugh Rivière. This picture belonged to Eliza Birchall

The Custom House, Venice, by J. Whitacre Allen

CHAPTER VII

Florence and Venice

Friday, 25 April. Today we have been renewing our memories of the glorious Pitti and Uffizzi and are just as much impressed by them as we were before we had seen Rome. Nothing can ever make the Seggiola or the Cardellino second-rate, they are unique in their special loveliness. But we do find the Venus di Medici (low be it spoken!) *less* beautiful than the Venus of Syracuse, and in some ways, than the Capitoline Venus, although the Medici *full*-face is perfect in its soft beauty. I was proud to show Dearman my pet walk from the Uffizzi to the Pitti, by the long passage over the Ponte Vecchio, for actually it was unknown to him, and he was delighted with the splendid etchings &c., by the old Masters, and the tapestries &c, there.

Saturday, 26 April. We saw the Arnolds yesterday in the Uffizzi. We came on by night train, leaving Florence at 7.15 and reaching Venice about 7 a.m., having for our only companions Capt. Hoole, (just turned up from Naples) and Sir Robert Abercrombie, both of whom were very pleasant. Capt. Hoole and we came together to Danieli's Hotel, which is *crowded,* but our rooms were ready for us. Unfortunately it is a wretched day, cold and raw and rainy, and beautiful Venice does not look like itself. We had a long prowl by land among the endless little paths, and over hundreds of the little bridges, ending up by losing ourselves completely, and having ignominious recourse to a gondola, when we found we were miles and miles from home.

Sunday, 27 April.   A dull wet cold morning – thick coats, sealskins and velvets in general requisition. We went to church and had the coldest dullest service I ever heard, *not one note of singing,* not even the Te Deum, not a single hymn, from beginning to end, service lessons, litany and Communion, all read in the same monotonous tones by the clergyman. And this with a *large* congregation of English ladies and gentlemen. We didn't feel drawn to go to the afternoon service after the morning's experience, so we took a walk, listening to the band in the Piazza &c., and then we rowed to the Public Gardens, the afternoon being bright and pleasant, so that Venice once more looked like itself, though it was still cold.

There is a party in this hotel whom we have seen once or twice before, and who perplex and amuse us considerably. They consist of a very pretty English girl, a nice quiet looking lady rather her senior, a fat old German gentleman, and a young English man. The latter has recognized Capt. Hoole as an old fellow-student in Germany, so now our curiosity as to the relations in which they all stand to one another is to some extent satisfied. The pretty girl is a young widow, only just 21, whose husband was killed out hunting a few months after their marriage. Though he has not been dead more than a year, the charming widow is dressed in the *very slightest* coquettish half-mourning, seems extremely lively, and flirts tremendously with the old German, who, unattractive though he is, attends her as her devoted shadow, and seems quite prepared to lay at her feet his portly person and the large fortune he has made in Australian sheep-farming. The other lady is her companion, and seems a very nice person. We fancy she is rather 'tired' by the levity of the widow. But what Capt. Hoole's friend has to do with them, and why the strange party all travel together, is still a mystery to Capt. Hoole and ourselves. Danieli's is crowded, and we have the largest company at the *table d'hôte* that we have had since the Grand Hotel Paris.

This morning we went out to eat ices in the Piazza, á la mode Venitienne, but it was quite too cold to sit out under the arcades; everyone took refuge within the cafes. As usual we see many Orientals of various nations, about the town.

Monday, 28 April. Capt. Hoole left this morning on his homeward journey; it was a great pity, for the day turned out charming, and he would have gained a far juster impression of Venice, had he remained. We had a long séance in Salviati's fascinating showrooms there. We wished to visit their 'fabrique' on Murano, but unfortunately the works are closed for repairs. However we did go over there, and were much interested in seeing some glass-making, though not Salviati's. We left Venice at 11 p.m. and had no end of trouble at the station, in consequence of the officials demanding gold for half the fares, and for the extra luggage, so Dearman had to rush off to get change, and with all their punctilios, we nearly lost the train.

Tuesday, 29 April. A weary long night journey, seven in the carriage, and no possibility of sleep, for whistles kept shrieking, and we stopped at all the stations. The train was so tremendously full, (all 1st class passengers) that we had the greatest difficulty in finding seats at all, and we reached Nabresina (where we ought to have had time for breakfast) a whole hour behind time. *We* stopped at Adelsburg, at 10.30, everybody else going on to Vienna. At Adelsburg, we found ourselves completely amid the snow, for there was a very heavy fall on Sunday; the first time we saw snow was at Lyons. Adelsburg is a nice fresh mountain village, surrounded by very beautiful scenery. The attraction, of course, is the gigantic Cave, which we went to visit as soon as we had breakfasted. We had it illuminated with 410 candles, and these are really necessary, as one would see practically nothing of it with mere torches carried in the hand. It is perfectly *enormous,* far far larger than I had expected (Dearman had seen it before). It took us $3\frac{1}{4}$ hours to make the round of it, walking all the time, and our guide was of opinion that at least as much more of this vast subterranean cavern yet remains to be discovered. Then its beauty is so great. I could not have conceived possible such endless variety of form in the glorious stalactites and stalagmites, pillars – of regular Corinthian forms, with fluted shafts and acanthus-decked capitals, – white wax candles, countless faithful representations of human beings, of birds, beasts and fishes, rich curtains, hanging in graceful folds as of yellow silk, and bordered with rich red fringes, festoons of striped ribbons, chairs, thrones, and pulpits, arches, colonnades, temples, 'the roof of Milan Cathedrals,' trees and plants, organs, and countless other curious and grotesquely accurate reproductions of all kinds of objects; these were in all colours, pure white, opaque, or perfectly transparent, rich yellow, and many shades of red, while some were covered with brilliant flashing diamonds. The weird beauty of these wonderful formations – ever varied, no two alike – combined with the rushing sound of the dark mountain torrent, that dashes along at the bottom of the largest hall, and with the deep boundless darkness looming round us beyond the range of the candle-flames, gave to the whole vast place a character almost unearthly.

Our guide gave us (for the trifling consideration of two gulden each) two insects, which he called Eliotorus, and which creep about, in blind darkness, on the stalactites, living on one knows not what. Of the blind Proteus Anguineus he very rarely sees a specimen, and he was surprised to hear that my brother had conveyed one to England, and kept it alive for a year. This evening we go to Gratz, our second consecutive night in the train, and we proceed to Vienna in the evening. We are running the Exhibition rather close.

Wednesday, 30 April. The first-class carriages last night were all so full that we found we could not travel with any hope of comfort, so we took possession of an empty *2nd class,* to the great amazement of the guard, who could not understand anyone in their senses preferring 2nd class to 1st, under any circumstances. We extended ourselves full-length on the seats, and slept very well, till we reached Marburg, when some people got out and left vacant a beautiful coupé, which we joyfully took possession of, and enjoyed till we reached Gratz at 9 a.m.

This is an extremely pretty place, and a flourishing and important town, the Capital of Styria.

We looked up our friend Capt. Morragh, whom we had seen at Venice on Sunday, and who preceded us to Gratz on Monday, as he 'can't stand night-journeys'. He is very much 'hipped', entertaining the conviction that he is the most delicate of men, and he caused us, at Sorrento and afterwards, great amusement by his piteous plaints of the *starvation* he underwent in Italy. He 'never had enough to eat' all the time he was in that miserable country. Vienna is the only place in the world where one can get decent food, and enough of it. Italy is a land of starvation, and he considers that Liebig's extract of meat actually saved his life, for he always kept a pot of it in his bedroom, and used to consume it in private. Now seeing that we beheld him every day at dinner help himself at least *twice* to every dish that was offered to him, we were always immensely amused by the perpetual pathetic descriptions he gave us of his wretched plight. But he is a *most pleasant* man; we like him exceedingly, and his hints about Austria have been very useful to us. He is wildly enthusiastic about Vienna and everything therewith connected, but he hates Italy.

Well, we looked him up at once, and he shewed us the beauties of Gratz, taking us up to the picturesque Schlossberg, whence we had a beautiful panorama. Capt. Morragh then joined us at luncheon, and saw us off at 4.15 in the train for Vienna. We had been gloomily anticipating to see every seat taken, and to be ignominiously left on the platform at Gratz, unable to get on to Vienna for the opening, but to our great surprize, and sincere pleasure, we found that there was abundance of room, and we were only three in our carriage. I suppose everybody had had the same idea of getting to Vienna in good time, so that the trains for some days before were crowded and now on the very *last* day, all the rush was over. It certainly was hardly prudent to time our arrival thus at the very last moment, and we should never have done it, had we not known that Oswald was on the spot here, to see that our room was kept for us. We saw the pass by daylight, and it is a most *wonderful* railway, ascending and descending 3000 ft. by sharp curves and zigzags, precipices yawning beneath, and the lofty mountains towering around.

CHAPTER VIII
Vienna Exhibition

Thursday, 1 May.   We reached Vienna at about ten last night and found at the station no omnibus, no cab, nothing but dainty little pair-horse broughams, quite unfitted for luggage. As we got in, I told our driver that we had *noch Gepäck* which announcement he took with equanimity, and we waited. By and bye I told him again, 'We have baggage you know – can you take it?' Oh yes, he could take it. But then second thoughts came, and he asked apprehensively 'Have you *much* luggage?' *'Ja, ziemlich viel* – we have 5 packages'. 'Not large ones,' anxiously – '3 rather large' 'what weight?' Dearman *'Drei hundert Pfund'* (300 lbs) *'Jesus Maria!!!'* in accents of such genuine horror that we could not help laughing. So it was arranged that a porter should convey the obnoxious *Gepäck,* on a hand-barrow, to our hotel – 2 miles off. (What a benighted way this seems, of receiving hordes of visitors, in a great city like Vienna!) Rather a dear way too, for we had to pay our driver three gulden, and the porter the same sum, our transfer from the station (which in Rome would have been 1/7d), here costing us 12/–. We found Oswald[21] awaiting us, and a good room on 3rd floor, the Manager having been 'utterly unable' to keep us rooms on the 1st, as he had promised Mr. Warburg. We should however be very comfortable, were it not for the trifling

---

[21] Oswald Birchell, Dearman's young cousin and partner.

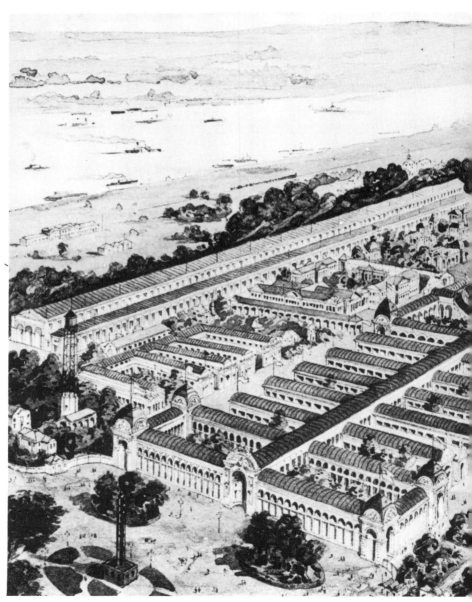

The Vienna Exhibition, 1873. (Photograph courtesy of H. Roger Viollet)

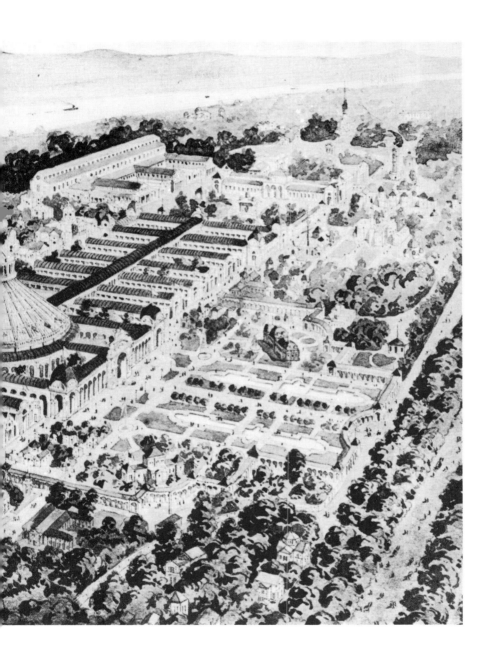

disadvantage that this large and well-furnished room contains no drawer, no hook, no hole or corner to put our things in, so we still live in our boxes, for every scrap of furniture in the house is in use, and all our representations are of no avail, though we meet with the utmost politeness and civility.

Vienna is crowded, not a bed to be had in the whole city, we hear, though several large new hotels have been built for the Exhibition. We like this hotel extremely; (the Goldenes Lamm, Leopoldstade) it is within an easy distance of the Exhibition, and is in every respect a thoroughly 1st rate house, food admirable in quality and perfect in cooking, waiters most obliging and strikingly good and respectable. Many English, many Japanese, a few Americans, and some Greeks, are staying in this Hotel.

The opening ceremony this morning was splendid and impressive, a sight not soon to be forgotten. But there was one *swindle* connected with it. We were led to believe that it was necessary to buy tickets at 50/– each, to see the opening, and it was expressly stated that no one not thus provided, would be admitted to the Rotunda. We afterwards found that, as a matter of fact, not only had all the exhibitors free access to the ceremony, without paying extra, but also thousands of people were admitted either gratuitously (which one would suppose from the appearance of some) or for a trifling fee, so that all those persons who had bought the 50/– tickets felt themselves immensely aggrieved.

One gentleman told us that he had never shewn his ticket at all, he *had* one of these 1st class ones, but he said he might just as well have had none, for he was never asked for it.

The seats were none of them numbered, though the tickets were, so instead of being marshalled, by obsequious officials, to our comfortable reserved places, we had to push among the crowd, and at last I found a chair, and Dearman secured capital vantage ground on the pedestal of a statue. We arrived at eleven, and found ourselves behind the majority of the visitors. The ceremony took place at 12 o'clock, the Emperor entering the hall, with the Crown Princess Victoria of England (as she is still called) on his arm, then the Empress with the Crown Prince, the Prince of Wales with the Princess of Coburg, the Crown Prince of Denmark, Prince Arthur (on his 23rd birthday) the young sons of the Emperor of Austria and of the Crown Prince of Prussia, the Count and Countess of Flanders, &c. &c. &c. The band played the Austrian National Anthem, then some speeches were made, the Emperor declared the Exhibition open, everybody cheered, and then the Royal party left the Rotunda to make the tour of the huge building, which occupied them more than an hour. They then returned to the Rotunda, and we saw them pass out close to us. The Emperor is a fine stately-looking man, worthy of the proud Hapsburgs, the Empress a lovely, graceful woman, of commanding height; the Crown Princess bonny and pleasant and cheerful, talking to the Emperor, and smiling to her friends in the crowd! Her husband grim, stolid and arrogant, standing forward stern and proud, and looking as if he were *the* figure of the day, never speaking, never smiling, considering evidently all the illustrious party around him as vastly inferior to himself. A greater contrast to his behaviour could not be imagined than that of our Prince of Wales, who was completely at his ease, pleasant, un-selfconscious, bright and cheerful, with a gentlemanly tact rather keeping in the background, and recognizing that he wasn't, on this occasion, the hero of the day, instead of thrusting himself obtrusively forward, like his brother-in-law. The ceremony was over, and the Royal party gone, by 3 p.m. The *uniforms* formed by far the most brilliant feature in the pageant; such variety, splendour and richness can surely be seen nowhere but in Austria.

All the Austrian officers were in their respective uniforms, and so were all the foreign 'gay militaries' present, the civilians

being in plain evening dress. The Hungarian magnates
appeared in dazzling magnificence, the Orientals, Turks,
Japanese, Persians, Egyptians, and a pig-tailed heathen
Chinese, wore their national costumes, and amid this blaze of
splendour, the ladies were nowhere, although the toilettes of
many would have excited notice and admiration anywhere else.

The Exhibition building is *vast*. It took us a quarter of an
hour to walk briskly across it, from end to end, but it is
wonderfully well-planned and clearly arranged. The Rotunda
is a very fine hall, of huge size and imposing form; it held
today at least 50,000.

Friday, 2 May.   We meant to go to the Exhibition early this
morning, but Dearman had a threatening of headache, so we
thought it was better to stay quietly indoors all the morning.
Our hotel has just been considerably enlarged, and is yet in a
very unfinished state, knocking going on continually,
workmen swarming, and some score or two of old women
whom we stumble over at every turn. They are always
sweeping the passages, or washing the stairs, or in other ways
laying pitfalls in our way. I believe the new rooms are very
damp still; ours is fortunately not new, though newly (and not
very completely) furnished.

We breakfast in it, but always dine in the beautiful, bright,
tastefully decorated dining-room.

Saturday, 3 May.   A long day at the Exhibition. Being an
expensive day, (admittance 10/- each) there were few visitors,
especially in the morning, but there were numbers of exhibitors and officials and thousands of workmen, for there are
10,000 at work by day, and 4,000 by night. The Exhibition
is in a deplorably unfinished state; some parts look perfectly
hopeless, and can certainly not be ready for months. One can
hardly yet form a fair idea of the merits of the various sections,

but one can compare their stages of completeness. Austria, the Orientals, Switzerland, and Germany are the most advanced; France, Italy and America the furthest *en retard*. Great Britain comes about midway. Her pottery is superb, and will be a most satisfactory show. The machinery is said to be admirable, but we have not seen it yet. But in regard to manufacturers, the English Exhibition is most disappointing. The things that are shown are good, but their quantity is very deficient, since hardly any of the large firms exhibit at all. Public spirit in England (and unfortunately above all in Leeds) seems lamentably wanting in this respect. And then the arrangement of the goods is wretched; utterly devoid of uniformity, totally regardless of general effect, and with no pretence at harmony of colour or form. England stands *absolutely* alone in the glorious distinction of *bad taste*.

The reason of the miserably bad effect of this part of the British department is that every man has been allowed to do that which was right in his own eyes, no stipulation being made as to size or shape of the cases, and consequently one sees ugly common yellow painted cases in the midst of the neat black picked out with gold, which is the prevailing colour, whilst the huge bare wooden back of a gigantic case stands gaunt and ugly behind a little squat box-like case, no attempt being made to hide the naked ugliness by flags or drapery. The very meanest, shabbiest case of all was sent by the Marshalls of Leeds!

Going from the British section to the tastefully arranged, harmonious Austrian department, or to the rich brilliance of the Orientals, one is filled with shame and confusion of face. It is lamentable that our great country, the originator of Exhibitions, should be behind Tunis and Portugal, Russia and Switzerland, in taste and perception of beauty. But the pottery department of the British section is admirable in every way, and it is most gratifying to see the very great improvement

England is making in this respect. We both together enjoy this department, and also the Eastern sections, but when Dearman buries himself in the contemplation of *cloth,* I go and study the *lace,* or feast my eyes on the splendid jewels, of fabulous value, exhibited in most of the sections.

Sunday, 4 May.   A dull cold wet day; the weather seems thoroughly unsettled, as yesterday was glorious. We overslept ourselves this morning, and were too late to go to the English service at the Embassy. In the afternoon, there being no service there, we went to the English church service in the Swiss church, a dark cold building, in the style of old-fashioned chapels. The service was as dull and frigid as the church, a congregation of nine persons, of whom no-one made the responses, save our three selves, and no singing whatsoever. From this we went into the noble gothic Cathedral, and the contrast was great, for here we found a very large congregation, all joining heartily in the beautiful singing, (even the old women singing with correctness of time and tune, though their voices were cracked) and then all listening attentively to an earnest and eloquent sermon.

Monday, 5 May.   A long day at the Exhibition, begun by buying some bog oak things at a stall kept by a very rosy cheeked Irish maiden, who informed us that 'it was myself packed the cases for the journey' — and wound up by a charming visit to the Oriental department. The Japanese, the Persians, the Tunisians, and above all the Turks, are coming out superbly, anything more gorgeous in colouring and arrangement, or more complete and exhaustive as an exhibition, than the Turkish department, it is impossible to conceive. This section, which occupies one entire wing of the building, is still closed to the public, as it is not quite finished, but we, being of an enterprising and irrepressible turn of mind, made general attacks on the door, in lofty disregard of the notice 'Verbotener Eingang' printed outside. Twice we were turned back, with the utmost politeness by the officer on guard, the third time we perceived a Turkish swell, the Secretary or something, in the distance. To him we made piteous pantomimic appeal, entreating to be admitted, and he, in the chivalry of his heart unable to refuse a lady, waves his hand deprecatingly, gives a reluctant assent, and we enter in triumph within the forbidden precincts, and were there fortunate to have this quiet opportunity of inspecting this most splendid collection of all the treasures of art and industry sent by this wonderful nation, now no sick man indeed, but a people vigorous, active and prosperous. The German soldiers on guard all touched their hats to us, as thinking we were some great ones; the Turks, working away in their native dress, only bestowed on us a glance of solemn stolidity, and went on with their work.

The walls are hung with brilliant flags, and rich warm carpets; all round the sides of the great gallery stand lay-figures wonderfully life-like, clad in all the various costumes of the land. More than a hundred of them: the cases are filled with the products of Turkey, but are not yet all complete. We spent part of this afternoon in the Persian department, and there, whilst Dearman was looking at carpets and rugs, and asking their prices, I was entertained by a most charming Oriental, the special envoy of the Court of Persia, who was most agreeable, intensely polite, and spoke French perfectly.

The number of things already sold is something wonderful, *all* the Persian carpets save one and of the beautiful sculptures which we so much admire, the five gems went off on the second day, bought by a Mr. Lewis who is *said* to be buying for the Halifax Crossleys.

Tuesday, 6 May. We had an admirable sight of the Crown Prince & Princess of Prussia and their son, of the Prince of Wales, and of Prince Arthur, all no end of swells, Lord & Lady Dudley, &c. yesterday in the English department. We remained near them for about ¾ of an hour, and as there was no crowd to speak of, and no formal clearing the way before them we were able to get quite close to them, each one in turn. The Prince of Wales was as genial and pleasant as possible, talking to the Exhibitors, or chatting with those around him, and speaking always with the clear refined tone, and absence of affectation, that distinguishes all our Royal Family. Prince Arthur looked as bright and lively as he did in Rome. I heard him once speaking German very well indeed, but otherwise the party all talked English, the Crown Princess with a decided foreign accent, more marked in her than in her German husband. She was dressed in a green silk dress, decidedly too keen in colour, which she held high up, exposing a foot and a half of white petticoat all round, a black mantle, and a black and white bonnet with some very ugly flowers; she was in a blue dress with pink bonnet on the opening day. She looked very nice and amiable, but she certainly does not dress well. She is excessively like the Queen, only of course much brighter looking. Her tall husband who towers above her round little figure, impressed us much more agreeably than on the opening day, and he unbent from his proud stiffness, and talked and smiled pleasantly, and his face lights up wonderfully when he smiles.

Today we met Capt. Morragh, in the Exhibition, so we asked him to dinner, and he dined with us this evening, and was most pleasant. He seems so thankful to have escaped with life from the starvation land of Italy, and to be back again in his beloved Vienna.

Wednesday, 7 May.   A glorious day, fine and hot. We spent it entirely at the Exhibition, being there from ten till six. We had a slight lunch at the Restaurant aux Trois Frères Provenceaux, and had the pleasure of paying 16/- for it!

We have explored the Park rather more today than we had done before, and we are charmed with its natural beauty, and with the picturesqueness of the buildings that are being put up in it, Swiss chalets, Turkish coffee-houses, and quaint Japanese erections, at which plebeian Japs in native dress are toiling hard, and from the summit of which floats, as flag, a huge canvas *fish*. We went through the *Blümen-austellung,* and found there a really *very fine* show of azaleas, calceolarias, cinnerarias, and rhododendrons, a fair show of roses, and a good one of pelargoniums. About a third of the space is devoted to fruit and vegetables; the apples are magnificent, and the large English strawberries are viewed with awe by the continentals, accustomed only to little wild strawberries. The German ladies congregate around the vegetables, and exclaim in ecstacy *'Was für Kartoffeln!'*[22] *'Ah! der wunderschöne Blümenkohl'*[23] &c.

We have an amicable divison of labour; whilst Dearman and Oswald are absorbed in *cloth,* I either gaze on the jewels, or else do point-lace. This afternoon I sat for an hour and a half engrossed with my hapless flounce, which has hardly been touched since I left England.

We are charmed (as who could help being?) with the Austrian bands. One playing in the Prater this afternoon, in the midst of an appreciative throng of all classes, was *delightful,* so delicate, so refined, so cultured. This evening we went to the Circus Renz. I believe it is considered about the finest circus in the world; it certainly is an admirable one, and I am still juvenile enough to have enjoyed the entertainment immensely. There was some very clever riding, jumping over flags, and through rings covered with paper, and so forth, by a fair equestrienne, there were amusing interludes by two 1st

[22] Potatoes.
[23] Cauliflower.

rate clowns, there were *exquisite* horses, trained to the highest
pitch of perfection, especially eight noble black arabs, who
really did everything but speak, there was an equestrian
quadrille, ridden by eight ladies and eight gentlemen, and
then the arena was cleverly transformed into a gay ball-room,
for the pantomine of Cinderella and it was very well done
indeed. Numbers of little boys were dressed up as swell
militaires, Bismark, Molike, Napoleon I, &c; three were
British Guardsmen, who made their appearance to the strains
of 'God Save the Queen', then later on the band played 'Rule
Britannia' and *John Bull* made his appearance, a fat little man
with wideawake hat, blue coat with brass buttons, gaiters,
and top-boots, who immediately proceeded, after bowing to
the Prince, to fall fast asleep, (the Austrian idea of an
Englishman, I suppose) to the great amusement of the
audience.

The programme concluded by a lion scene; eight fright-
fully ferocious lions in a huge cage, to whom entered the
great lion tamer Delmonico, a negro, gorgeously clad in
green satin. The furious animals roared horribly, sprang
about, dashed round him, and seemed every moment about
to spring on him, but he had marvellous command over
them, and at a gesture from him they all cowered down at
the end of the cage. It all looked fearfully dangerous, though,
and so did a Japanese performance earlier in the evening,
high in the air, not on a *tight rope* but on a loose shaking
cord, and with nothing on the ground to break the fall, in
case of accident.

Thursday, 8 May. We had an amusing rencontre in the
Exhibition yesterday, meeting a lady and gentleman, of whom
the latter suddenly stopped, saying 'Oh! here is Mr. Birchall'
and they and he shook hands, and talked for some minutes
most amicably, they said they had seen us in church at Venice.

When they had said goodbye and gone on, I asked Dearman why he had not introduced me to his friends, when he replied that he had not the *faintest idea* who they were; but had not the courage to confess his ignorance to them! They were both quite young, and looked nice. We hear today that Amy has a little boy born on the 5th, and little Elsie is not yet a year old, and very delicate.

Dearman has been busy today superintending the hanging of his 'goods', so I did not go to the Exhibition till after lunch, and was thankful to have a little time for writing.

Friday, 9 May. A *drenching* wet day, cold, gloomy and altogether depressing. Nevertheless we went to the Exhibition, driving thither of course, but when we came away, by the usual brilliant arrangement, there was not the ghost of a carriage to be had for love or money, and thousands of people, ourselves among them, had to walk though *seas* of such mud as I never before personally experienced, for the unfinished state of the Exhibition park, makes it, in wet weather, a perfect *slough of despond.* My white petticoat was *soaked* with dirty moisture and encrusted with grey mire for more than a foot up, and I was obliged, when I reached home, to change *everything* I had on.

The great flaw in the Exhibition arrangement is this stupid rule of allowing no carriage to come within its enormously extensive precints.

Saturday, 10 May. The Exhibition as usual. By way of a change we determined to *dine* there, as we had to go out in the evening, so we dined at 2 o'clock chez les 'trois Frères Provenceaux' which was crowded. Then I went to the Indian department, and was perfectly charmed with the *lovely* gold and silver jewellery, especially with a most exquisite necklace of gold coins, price £50.

Dearman and I left the Exhibition earlier than usual, and went to the Grand Hotel, where we found by the visitors' book that the mysterious lady and gentleman of Thursday were the Cleverly Alexanders, of Haringay. So we left cards for them, and then did the same at the Jockey Club for Capt. Morragh. At 7.30 we went to an entertainment recommended by Mr. Warburg, a Concert given by four Swedish ladies, who are making a tour, and singing quartettes, chiefly Swedish airs, *most charmingly*. We were both of us perfectly delighted with the entertainment, there was something so especially refined, and so different from ordinary concerts, about it. The ladies are all remarkably pleasant looking, modest and simple in manner, all dressed alike in white muslin, and have all of them beautiful voices very highly cultivated. One song, in which they sang first the air, and then an exquisite distant echo of it, was I think about the most charming thing I ever heard. The audience were intensely appreciative, listening in absolute silence, and then at the close of each song, bursting into a torrent of applause. The fair quartette had a perfect ovation, being called before the audience more than twenty times, and *obliged* to repeat nearly every song, and then at the end the people all stood up, and cheered them *wildly* for at least a quarter of an hour, 'Bravo' and 'Hoch' shouted by each one of the crowd.

Sunday, 11 May.   This broken weather seems as if it would not settle down into fine days and bright sunshine. This we have one day, and then the next we are shivering with cold and drenched with rain. We ought not to murmur after our three months of summer, but we do find it very tiresome and disappointing.

We went to the Embassy church this morning. It is not large and was extremely full; fortunately we were very early. We met the Alexanders, and walked home with them, and at five we went to dine at the Grand Hotel (though not as their guests) and they went with us to hear the music in the Volksgarten afterwards.

We are more and more charmed with Vienna; today the afternoon was hot and brilliant, after a dull cold morning, and the Ringstrasse, the gardens, and the part about the Hof, were most charming.

Monday, 12 May. Most of the day was, as usual, spent at the Exhibition. The state of things there really seems to grow worse, instead of better; the Rotunda becomes daily more and more filled with packing cases, ladders, scaffolding, and workmen, and the noise of hammers resounds in every department. The French are really working in earnest now, and their cases, when finished, will be about the best, in respect of taste and richness, in the Exhibition. The Germans have today opened out a splendid collection of Dresden China, in a gorgeous Chinese-pagoda-like case. It seems inevitable that many man weeks must elapse before the Exhibition is really finished, and of course it is to the workmen's interest to prolong the work as much as possible, especially when they are being paid 3/6 an hour, which we know some in the English section are receiving.

The Alexanders dined with us this evening, and were very pleasant. They came up to our room after dinner.

Tuesday, 13 May. This miserable unsettled weather seems as if it never would go away. Last night our hopes rose high, for after a storm of thunder and vivid lightning, we had a lovely clear moonlight evening, without a cloud in the sky. But this morning all is again unsettled, fine gleams alternating with rain, and it is quite cold. The English princes are at Pest, and we wonder how they enjoy their great regatta under these circumstances.

We tried the Russian restaurant today, and found our lunch excessively dear; a single beefsteak cost 3/6! and the rest at the same rate. It is little frequented, and no wonder, in spite of its picturesque waiters in blue and pink.

This evening Dearman and Oswald have been at the Exhibitors' dinner, which was a very swell affair, fine old wines, and every delicacy conceivable, dinner lasting from 6 to 10.30.

Earl Cowper was in the chair, in the absence of the Prince of Wales.

Wednesday, 14 May. I don't think I have ever related the sequel to our discreditable affair with the Roman ferry man, when we never paid our fares. These amounted to 1d for the two of us, and all the time we were in Naples the unpaid debt weighed on my mind. So when we returned to Rome, I persuaded Dearman one day that we were near the ferry, to go and give the man ½ a franc, and to explain to him that we owed him part of it for unpaid fare. I told Dearman how to say this in Italian, which however he straightway forgot. When he arrived at the place, the boat was half way across, on its way to the opposite bank, but the boatman, seeing a gentleman rushing frantically down the steps, politely put back to shore to accommodate the belated customer. What was his surprize, when instead of getting into the boat, Dearman put into his hand a 50 centesimi note! The man stared and asked an explanation, the passengers all stared, a little crowd collected at the landing place, and stared too, Dearman endeavoured to explain in English, aided by Italian gesticulations; the situation was, he says, embarrassing in the extreme. At last the boatman seemed to comprehend that the half franc was now his property, though why he could not conceive, so he pocketed it, poured forth a volume of thanks, and then Dearman made his escape, conscious that they all regarded him as a benevolent lunatic with a mania for almsgiving, apprehensive of being followed and placed under medical surveillance, yet feeling in his heart the peace of a good conscience, and satisfied that the poor had now his own again – with a very good percentage of interest added on to it.

Today Dearman has bought some lovely Persian rugs etc. We dined this evening with the Alexanders, at the Grand Hotel and had a pleasant evening.

Thursday, 15 May. A long morning, chiefly spent with the Alexanders, in the Persian department, where I enjoyed much agreeable converse with my special friend, the Persian envoy, Petros Khan and a very nice Turk, a friend of his, named Hassan Merzeh, whilst Dearman bought Persian rugs right and left, and Mr. Alexander looked on, demeaning himself with infinite caution, till at last the spirit of acquisitiveness seemed to take possession of him, and he rushed into the mêlée to follow suit with a reckless eagerness far surpassing that of Dearman. Oswald left Vienna for England this afternoon.

We went to the Opera in the evening, and saw 'Sardanapol' a *gorgeous* tableau, the dresses, scenery, and whole *mise en scène* a perfect *dream* of brilliant splendour. We were delighted with the charming beauty of the much vaunted House. The Emperor and Prince Arthur were there.

Friday, 16 May. A glorious day at last, and the bright hot sunshine tempted out thousands of people to the Exhibition, so that it was about the gayest day we have had. Besides the Alexanders and Capt. Morragh we saw the Beckett Denisons, Capt. Alfred Drummond, and my old friend Fraulein Bernhard, now married, it appears. This was the day of the opening by the Emperor of the *'Kunsthalle'* and the crowd

there in the afternoon was tremendous. We saw the Crown
Prince and Princess of Prussia pushing their way among the
crowd.

We went through the English Machinery and Agricultural
Implements today, and I was surprised to see in the latter
section, small cases containing Brown & Polson's, Fry's and
Huntley & Palmers'[24] wares among the huge threshing,
reaping and rolling engines of John Fowler & Co. Verily the
arrangement of the English department here is remarkable!

---

[24] Cornflower, cocoa, chocolate, and biscuits.

CHAPTER IX

Budapest

Saturday, 17 May. Young Mr. Lawson, of Leeds, dined with us last night; he is a friend of Oswald's and has been very kind to him here. He is exhibiting largely in the machinery department and tells a lamentable tale of the delays and annoyances he has encountered. It was a very great mistake on the part of the Austrian railway companies, to undertake, unassisted, the huge labour of conveying all the vast quantities of goods to Vienna. Whole bales of them are stranded somewhere between Antwerp and Vienna, and their luckless owners cannot even learn their whereabouts.

Today we have had a charming trip down the Danube, from Vienna to Pest,[25] passing the battle-fields of Wagram and Essling and the towns of Presburg,[26] with its castle and race course, Komaram, red-towered and picturesque, Gran[27] with its large and magnificently situated Cathedral, the dome of which is built after the model of S. Peter's at Rome, and dozens of pretty country towns and hamlets. The real Danube river is reached, in a small steamer, by means of the Donau Canal, in about half an hour from Vienna. It is in parts enormously wide, in parts divided into several channels,

[25] Budapest.
[26] Bratislava.
[27] Esztergoin.

forming picturesque islands, one of which is as much as 55 miles in length. The river scenery as far as Presburg (2½ hours from Vienna) is extremely beautiful; beyond Presburg it is comparatively flat and tame, though richly-wooded all the way, then before Waitzen[28] the hills come close up to the river's edge, and the scenery is charming, and lastly, the immediate approach to Pest, passing the lovely Margarethen is very pretty indeed.

We left Vienna at 6.30, and reached Pest about 7.30, after a glorious day, for the weather is splendid again today, happily, and most favourable to our excursion. The large steamer we entered on reaching the Danube proper was well-filled, the 1st class part containing Italians, Wallachians, Hungarians, Austrians, Germans and English, the steerage, a most picturesque crowd of natives, the wildest-looking set we ever saw, with long fair moustaches, huge pipes, garments of undressed sheep skin, boots of cowhide, or bare feet, below the wide Turkish trousers, and language the strangest in Europe. One of the native Hungarians, a nobleman, was the greatest swell on board, clad in the national dress, tight coat covered with rich embroidery, tassels and bows, with scores of cornelian buttons, soft hat with bright feathers, tight blue trousers, and huge boots up to the knee, his enormously long meerschaum in his mouth, whilst his splendid beard and handsome features made him a most picturesque figure. Two 'fat red priests' sat next to us at our early *table d'hôte,* talking pleasantly to the rest of the company in half the languages of Europe, and enjoying their victuals with a zest quite wonderful to behold; they wear small beaver hats of the secular shape.

Sunday, 18 May.   The whole of this part of Pest seems to have undergone great changes recently. The maps and descriptions

---

[28] Vacz.

in Baedeker make the Hotel Queen of England *on the Danube,*
but we, innocently driving to it last night, found it all
among streets, and a long way back from the river, with no
view at all. We thought it would be suicidal to spend our
time at Pest out of sight of the Danube, so we calmly told
the obsequious porter and waiters who rushed eagerly out to
welcome us, that we had made a mistake, we must be in a
hotel close to the river, whereupon they most politely
directed us to the Grand Hotel Hungaria, which we found to
be quite new, close to the river, and very handsome and
refined in all its appointments, by far the finest hotel we have
seen save in Paris or Vienna, beating the best hotels in
much-frequented Italy hollow, though it is far in the heart of
Hungary!

This Hungarian language baffles me completely, for the
first time I am in a country where I know absolutely *not one
syllable* of the language, and *such* a language it is! It does not
sound so bad as it looks, in fact it really strikes one's ear as a
rather soft and pleasant kind of speech, but the words over
the shops, and in the newspapers, look dreadful. I have a
paper now before my eyes, in which I chance to see the words
'könyokereskedo' 'megszerezhetok' 'Zubszótár' 'okzerüzeggel',
'Könzakiaóhiratalahaü, 'Savogyogy aszat', 'fürdöizazatósáztól,'
&c. &c. all these in one half page, and hundreds, longer and
more uncouth-looking, to be easily found.

We have been much amused in our attempts to extract
some meaning out of the barbarous Hungarian newspapers,
to see the frequent (and so far as we could judge, always
complimentary) mention of 'A *Walesi Kerczeg*' (the Prince of
Wales) & '*A Arthur Kerczeg*'. (The Prince Arthur).

Our Princes seem to have made themselves extremely
popular in Pest, and everyone is full of admiring remarks
about them, and ancedotes of their visit, whilst the beauty of
Lady Dudley seems to have made quite a sensation here.

Prince Arthur has had only the *lesser* lion's part to play in
Vienna and Pest, his elder brother engrossing perhaps more
attention, and having more to do. Poor Prince Arthur used
to get dreadfully tired in Rome, we heard, hunting all day,
or else vigorously sight-seeing, then a great dinner, and then
every night one or more balls, and these he could never leave
till after the Princess Margharita had taken her departure,
and seeing that she never did so, till very late, the poor
youth had a hard time of it, and on one occasion is said to
have actually fallen asleep, standing, in the middle of a
cotillion! The gracious Princess kindly pretended not to
observe this.

Many stories are current respecting the Duke of Edinburgh
and his love affairs. One, which I have on good authority, is
that he met the Grand-Duchess two years ago at Hesse
Darmstadt, when both were visiting the Princess Alice. He
fell desperately in love with her, and proposed for her; the Czar
did not dislike the idea of the connection, but the Empress
made diligent enquiry into the Prince's character, found out
that he was somewhat wild, particularly with respect to
gambling, and put him on a year's probation before letting the
affair go any further. He was very steady indeed till nearly the
end of the time, but then at last he yielded to temptation, and
began to play again. Another year's trial was granted him, he
has passed it triumphantly, and has been allowed to pursue his
courtship at Sorrento.

Whether this story be entirely true or not, everyone seems
agreed in one point, that it will be, on both sides, a real love
match.

We had such an amusing experience this morning. We
walked over the long and graceful suspension bridge, to the
old town of Ofen, or Buda, without any special purpose, only
the general one of 'taking a look round'. There we saw before
us at some distance a railway line, with carriages *ascending* and

descending, apparently going straight up the face of the hill on which stands the Royal Palace, &c. of Ofen. We wondered much, and went towards it, till we found ourselves in a sort of little station, where without speaking a word, Dearman took 2 tickets, paying for them about 10 *kreugers* each, and we took our seats in what looked like an ordinary railway carriage though we were really in the lowest compartment of a cable car. The door was shut, and we began to rise in the air as it seemed. It felt somewhat like going up in a balloon would, I fancy, and was very pleasant and novel. In about a minute we found ourselves at the top of the steep hill, the small train stopped without the slightest jerk, and we got out. We found it too hot to walk much, so after quietly enjoying the beautiful views for some time, we returned to the station, found a 'train' all ready for us, entered the lowest carriage, and descended. It was far more peculiar than the ascent had been, for we felt as if we were sinking down, down, into nothingness, like one does in nightmare dreams, and I half anticipated a horrible crash when we touched the ground. But nothing came, we reached the bottom, came to a stand in peace, and gave up our cheap little return tickets. This a charmingly easy way of surmounting a steep hill, and it seems capitally managed. Of course it is worked by an engine and rope, and there is an up and down train every five minutes. Like the Monte Cenis, this Ofen hill has not only a railway over it, but also a tunnel through it, which is much used, especially by carriages. The Pest and Ofen Suspension bridge is well-conducted, passengers to Ofen go to the right, those to Pest to the left, so there is no confusion. A toll of 2 kreugers is paid at one end, a metal check received, and given up at the other end. The good people of Hungary seem to be hyper-particular on some points. This afternoon I was walking in the street, and slightly holding up my dress at the back, as the road was very dusty. I saw one or two people staring rather at me, but attributed it to interest in the general foreignness of our appearance, when a woman who had just passed us, turned back to me, and with many polite remarks in Hungarian, proceeded to pull down my dress all round, evidently totally ignorant that I had been *holding it up* and thinking I was quite unconscious of the very disorderly state of my garments. It is *comme-il-faut* here to always trail one's dress.

Monday, 19 May. Another glorious day, and Dearman's head, which was dreadfully bad all yesterday and the day before, being much better, we spent a delightful morning. First we went over to Buda, and ascended the Blocksberg, the fortress crowned hill to the left of the town, and a short cut recommended to us in preference to the winding carriage-road, led us through all the back slums of Ofen, which cluster up the sides of the Blocksberg, and here the odours were so pestiferous, drainage apparently being a thing unknown, that we both thought it would be a highly favourable place for the development of cholera, and an hour or two afterwards I read in the *Leeds Mercury* (we hear nothing of it here) that this disease is *even now raging* in Pest and Buda! No wonder I am sure.

We greatly enjoyed the splendid view of both towns, the Danube, the flat country behind Pest, and the mountains towards Vienna from the summit of the Blocksberg, and then we rejoined the carriage (which was waiting below for us) and took a drive all round Pest. We were greatly struck by the evident prosperity of the city. Large handsome houses in wide new streets are springing up on all sides, and the new buildings already finished are extremely fine.

We went into the Museum, and were interested in seeing the close attention given to the things by working men during their dinner hour, peasants from the far interior, and Pesthians of all classes. We were, apparently, the only foreigners.

We left Pest at 1.25 and stopped at 6 p.m. to dine at Presburg, going on in the evening to Vienna, where we received quite a warm welcome back at the Goldenes Lamm from Manager, porter, waiters and chambermaids, the latter vociferous with their *'Küss die Hand'*.

CHAPTER X
Vienna

Tuesday, 20 May. This Hotel is a strange mixture. The downstairs department is perfect, a smiling and gentlemanly manager; a clerk in whom Dearman finds quite a congenial spirit; a porter who is intelligent and civil as could be; two small boys in buttons, who pull off their caps and stamp our letters and say 'Guten Morgen' in their patois; waiters whose respectability, attention and civility are all that can be desired, and numerous other officials who take off their hats to us, but whose other duties I fail to perceive. Upstairs, *au troisième*, we have a young waiter who is the acme of politeness, and appears at 6 a.m. in immaculate black clothes and white tie, but who brings us breakfast always half an hour late, and answers the bell when it suits him, we have three chambermaids, evidently country girls just caught for the Exhibition, (for we are on the edge of the new part of the house, and are waited on by the new staff) who are lively, pretty, pleasant and respectful, who never see us without a curtsey and a 'Küss die Hand' who never by any chance bring us towels of their own free will, who have only once brought us some tepid water in the morning, though we nightly request them to furnish us with *Heisses Wasser* every morning, at least we did do for the 1st 3 weeks, and now, in despair, we have dropped the subject; we have a 'boots' who like all the rest, is civility itself, but who certainly only looks at our boots — never cleans them. We have a handsome washerwoman, wealthy, by reason of her exorbitant charges, who brings home the linen in neat cases of basket-work, in a large waggon drawn by a pair of beautiful carriage horses, and sends her husband round to the rooms with the things; last, not least, we have a Wandering Lunatic, who never does anything at all, but meanders about on all the floors, and peeps at one round every unsuspected corner.

Wednesday, 21 May. The American ladies we met at the Italie in Rome, Mrs. and Miss Crow and Miss Dewy, with a young Mr. Crow, fresh from Japan, are now here, on the same storey as we are. I go in every morning to sit a while with Miss Crow, who is extremely delicate, and I go and see them every evening too.

Today we have, as usual, spent most of our time at the Exhibition, especially in the Kunsthalle. The English pictures are *first-rate,* there are not very many of them, but every one is good, and there is a great variety, a superb Turner; and to me the best known of all pictures is here, Sir E. Landseer's splendid old *Sanctuary,* Davis' *Moonrise,* Millais' *Three Sisters,* and *Nina Lehmann;* Hook's *Hoisting Sail;* and Frith's *Ramsgate Sands,* these and many more of our finest modern paintings are here. The English watercolours we have not yet seen, — I fancy there are not many.

Thursday, 22 May. We dined last night at Sacher's Restaurant, near the Grand Opera, and found it a capital place, and hardly so dear as our usual dining-place, our own hotel, for, contrary to the Vienna custom, we nearly always dine in the Goldenes Lamm, *Speise-saal.*

This being Ascension Day, is kept as a general holiday here, shops all closed, and Exhibition only 1/– admission (the same as Sundays). We went in to the Cathedral this morning, and heard some exquisite singing. Afterwards we went to the

Picture Gallery of the Belvedere, and were delighted with the Rembrants, the *Ruisdaels,* the Van Dycks, some very fair Rubenses, and some landscapes by David Teniers. We went to the Exhibition in the afternoon, and it was *crowded,* too much so for our comfort.

Friday, 23 May.   Isabel Crow came and sat with me all the morning, whilst Dearman was busy in the town. He brought home Mr. Rack to lunch with us and then we went to the Exhibition.

We are rather amused to see what a sensation the Vienna panic is making in England, for *here* we hear and see nothing of it. The 'hundred failures a day' are those of mere petty speculators, mad adventurers, and their downfall seems to be regarded as rather a good thing than otherwise, and no one of any importance has come to grief. The Jews are somehow blamed for the wild rage for speculation which has caused the crash, and are in very bad odour just now. We passed their handsome synagogue today; it is completely surrounded by the dwellings of Israelites and house-doors, shops, and signboards are all surmounted by cabalistic Hebrew characters. It is strange to see a pawn-shop adorned by the grand old mysterious signs.

Saturday, 24 May.   The Crows leave today for Dresden. Isabel has only been able to visit the Exhibition once, when she was wheeled round in a chair, and then she took cold, poor girl, and has since remained in the house.

After a short visit to the Exhibition this afternoon, we had a charming drive, right away to the end of the Prater, and then we told the man we wanted to see the Danube (as if we hadn't already seen it abundantly!) so he turned out of the road and drove us along a grassy sward among the trees, till we came to a regular *cul de sac,* whence no possible exit appeared. Here he stopped, dismounted and told us we must ascend a high steep embankment of stones and pebbles, which we did with no small exertion, and then we found ourselves in a vast plain of these said pebbles, tracked in all directions by lines of railway, with the *main line* high above us, crossing the broad river on a new and very beautiful bridge. We walked across the strange land of stones, till we came (after crossing half a dozen railways) to the very brink of the Danube itself, and here the view all round was lovely, and the huge mighty river, flowing past at our feet, very grand indeed, though why the music named in its honour is called 'The Beautiful *Blue* Danube' passes our comprehension, for the water is scarcely bluer than that of the Tiber. We had been at first puzzled by the strange scene immediately around us, but soon perceived a great dredging machine at work in the water close to the banks, bringing up waggons-ful by the score of river mud and pebbles, which was immediately carried away by the various railways. There were so many of these, that we really felt in peril of our life, for engines kept coming round corners straight down upon us, and whilst we gazed at a long passenger train crossing the bridge above us, we were warned by the pointsman's shout that we were standing just in the way of a train full of stones coming from the dredger. This wonderful machine has brought up from the river bed all the vast mass we were walking on, and the rails that perplexed us at first, have been made for the sole purpose, apparently, of conveying the pebbles away, to the edge of the embankment, which they are thus constantly augmenting.

We went this evening to the Hofoper theatre to hear *Il Trovatore;* it was a capital performance, *all* the singing good, and the band admirable, and the house is *exquisite.* We saw not one single person whom we knew.

Both our Princes have left Vienna, after being received by the people and entertained by the Emperor, right royally, and the King of the Belgians arrived last night, the first of the Crowned Heads to appear.

Sunday, 25 May. I said some time ago that the great drawback to the Exhibition was the difficulty of getting a carriage to bring one home. I ought to modify this remark. There are dozens of tramway cars, running from the West entrance of the Exhibition to the town, and these are most convenient and very comfortable; we tried one one day, and found it infinitely *more select* than we had expected. The rush at these cars on a wet day, is amusing to witness. Then if you engaged a carriage to bring you back, it must wait all the time, you cannot say 'Go away and come back at such an hour', but it may not wait at the *door*. The carriages all stand some distance from the Exhibition, and when one is wanted, it is telegraphed for, a wire having been placed on purpose, from the Exhibition doors to the Stand, and a numbered ticket being given on arrival to both coachmen and owner or 'fare', as the case may be. This is an excellent plan, and works well, so that the only *real* difficulty is in the case when one has not engaged a carriage beforehand. *Then,* since no carriage is allowed to enter the Park, one has certainly to walk a long way and probably all the way home, as it is most difficult to find a carriage of any sort.

The Orientals in Vienna increase in number and variety. At the Exhibition Copts and Nubians, Armenians, Japanese, Persians and Negroes, abound, and yesterday a most gorgeous swell was there, resplendant in gold and jewels and costly array, a diamond covered tobacco box in his hand, and a belt of large diamonds flashing around his shoulders and waist. He was a Persian, and suffered sorely, poor man, from the attentions of the crowd who collected round him. The habitués of the Weltausstellung are used to much that is novel and brilliant, but this even moved them to curiosity and admiration.

Our hotel is decidedly the favourite one for Oriental potentates, and since we have been here Royal carriages have waited at the door almost every day whilst their occupants were doing honour to the grandees staying in the house, but the greatest sensation has been produced today. H.R.H. the Prince of Montenegro is here, attended by fourteen armed Orientals, in gorgeous attire, with fierce wild faces, and their hands constantly grasping their sword, as they guard their Prince's person, drawn up around the door of his room. We failed to see him this morning, but each of his retainers might have been a prince, to judge from his appearance. All day the greatest swells of Vienna have been calling here to pay their devoirs to the illustrious Oriental, the stairs have swarmed with Royal footmen, in plumes and cocked hats, and the entrance-hall has been filled with an eager crowd of spectators. *We* have not been indoors much, for we took a carriage for the day (£2.2.0), and have used it a good deal. First we went to the Augustiner Church, and heard part of the High Mass, most beautifully sung, and then we went at 11.30 to the English service at the Embassy, where we had a very good sermon. We saw no one we know, except Mr. Royle, of the Indian Department.

This afternoon we drove to Schönbrunn, and much enjoyed strolling about the lovely grounds, which are immensely large, and beautifully wooded. There were hosts of people; it is a delightful thing for the Viennese to have such a charming place for their Sunday afternoon promenade, and so near too, only about two miles away.

After our return from Schönbrunn, we were so fortunate as to meet all the swells coming from the Races; first the Empress, in a carriage and four with outriders, then the Emperor, with the King of the Belgians at his side, and then the usual swarms of Archdukes.

Monday, 26 May. The Exhibition buildings in the park here are most interesting, so far at least as one can at present judge, for very few are finished. Besides all the regular restaurants of the different nations, there is a charming Turkish Coffee house, where we took some coffee most festively the other day. We were waited on by gorgeous Turks clad in brilliant national costumes, who gave us coffee in sweet little cups minus handles, but in silver holders, whilst around us Germans, Italians and Englishmen were diligently trying to smoke tchibouks and narghiles,[29] and one or two Turkish gentlemen doing so 'quite spontaneously' and watching with evident amusement, the praiseworthy efforts of the neophytes. The Japanese tea-house is all but finished, and is very charming. Little artificial ponds, in which are kept tortoises, fastened to stones to prevent their straying, pretty bridges, native houses with paper walls, Japanese wares of all kinds, Chinese lanterns festooned all round, blue China everywhere, Native Japs of every age and every rank, while over all floats the huge fish, the national flag of this strange country. One night last week a dozen of the Japs who are staying in this house had Baron Schwarz, the pleasant genial English-looking Director of the Exhibition, to dine with them and they seemed to be a very cheerful party. There is one very fat rosy Jap who amuses us immensely by his keen sense of humour. He is perpetually dissolved in inextinguishable laughter, so infectious that we can hardly look at him without laughing too.

The Viceroy of Egypt is building a pavilion for the reception of himself, and suite when he comes to the Exhibition, and so is the Prince of the Sovereign State of Monaco. There is to be also in the Park, an Exhibition of Children's Toys, but this unfortunately we shall not see, as it opens only on the 15th of June.

---

[29] Oriental tobacco pipes with smoke passed through water.

Thursday, 29 May. I saw in the Fremdentblatt this morning the name of 'Herr Elias Howart, Ingénieur, London, in which I at once recognized an attempt at Eliot Howard, whom we had been looking out for for some days. So we called on him this afternoon, at the large new Hotel Donau, where he is staying, and asked him to dine with us tonight, but he was unfortunately engaged so we have appointed to meet at the Exhibition tomorrow. Without some such appointment, there are thousands of chances against one's meeting people. Eliot has been here since Saturday, but we had never seen him, though he and we have spent nearly all our time at the Exhibition.

Yesterday we met Mr., Mrs. and Miss Rhodes, of Leeds, and Harry Hudson, the first buying enamels and bronzes with vigour, the latter on his way home from the East. English people seem beginning to come in greater numbers, we have seen more British faces during the last few days than ever during our stay here. The English 'swells' have most of them departed, but Lord and Lady Dudley are still in Vienna. As soon as they leave, Hancock's are going to exhibit the Countess' splendid jewels, which they brought here for her, £300,000 worth, and as they have on show £200,000 of their own, they had to bring £500,000 worth of jewels from London to Vienna. They engaged a coupé for the whole journey, and had two detectives to guard the precious strong-boxes, besides their own two men, and the man who told me about it said that he himself had never left the case since it arrived, he had not even seen the Rotunda! He says Lady Dudley never travels with her jewels, and here she does not even have it with her, for every evening one of Hancock's men takes up the parure she has selected for that night's wear, to the Imperial Hotel, where she is staying. Lord Dudley has bought a good many things in the Exhibition, but not to quite so large extent as Sir Richard Wallace.[30]

---

[30] Of the Wallace Collection.

We are surprised to see how little the Prince of Wales has done in the way of making purchases. The only thing to which I have seen his name attached, is a set of Minton's small cups and saucers. It was observed, the day he went all through the English section with the Crown Princess of Prussia, that several times when he seemed on the point of buying something, she checked him, by whispering that it was very dear, or that it would be of no use to him; by reason of this economical plan of action, both for herself and her brother, she was not very popular with the Exhibitors. She has the character of being exceedingly economical in everything. Prince Arthur bought a Persian rug − rather an odd choice for a young bachelor, it seemed to us.

We have made great efforts to secure some of the charming Indian things, and have for that purpose interviewed Mr. Rolfe, Capt. Walker, and Mr. Clarke. The latter is most kind, and has promised to do all he can for us; the things are not yet on sale.

Wednesday, 28 May. We met Eliot at 10 this morning and I had a very pleasant stroll round the sections with him for two hours, whilst Dearman was busy buying 'Dresden', and performing other business of an equally important nature. In the meantime he met Mr. Stanfield and Mr. Moorsom, to my very great sorrow, when I found that I had missed seeing the latter.

We have quite an *affecting* parting today from our friend Petros Khan, who seemed heart-broken at the thought of seeing us no more, and a very friendly one from Mr. Clarke.

This afternoon we went to the Museum, a very fine building, the inner court decorated like Pompeii or the Loggie at the Vatican, and then we ascended the steeple of the grand old Cathedral (and witnessed, *en passant,* a gorgeous funeral) and, finally, we took a drive in the Prater, by way of bidding adieu to those miles of splendid blooming chestnuts, and that gay scene of life and brightness.

The splendid Persian whom we saw the other day, sparkling with diamonds and brilliant colour, turned out to be no less a person than the *uncle* of the Shah, now resident in Russia. Having observed that he had a fair, rather florid complexion, and red hair and beard, I asked my friend Petros Khan whether this was not rare among Persians. He told me that it was not the pure Persian type at all, but was characteristic of the Royal Family, who were of mixed Persian, Circassian, and Mongolian descent. Speaking of the Shah, he said that the Monarch is personally of an avaricious turn, and that whatever may be the expenses of this great Westward Progress, His Majesty will take care not to increase them by lavish prodigality. The Khedive, on the contrary, squanders money for the mere pleasure of the thing, and throws gold coins by the thousand broadcast in the streets. We heard a most extraordinary account of the mad extravagance in Cairo at the late Royal Marriages.

Thursday, 29 May.   This day we left Vienna, after a very pleasant month's sojourn in the beautiful city, marred only by the almost incessant bad weather we have had.

We had a busy morning, winding up our affairs in general, and performing the other complicated operation of packing, apportioning one box for the journey, others to be left at the stations, one box for things not wanted in London, to be sent direct to Gloucester, and the rest for London. We had 'tipped' profusely in our Hotel, so we left in the odour of sanctity, having, as Dearman said, done our best to 'gild the Lamb'. We have seen in the English newspapers the absurdest statements as to its being possible to dine in Vienna at one gulden, or even less. It *may* be – at 3rd class eating-houses, but certainly in none of the places that the ordinary run of visitors would frequent. In the good restaurants, the very lowest fixed price for a dinner is 3 florins, without wine, and dining *à la carte* is of course very much more expensive. The few Hotels which have a *table d'hôte,* charge 3½ florins for it, without wine; our simple little dinners at the Goldenes Lamm, come to about 12/– each every evening; one slight lunch at the Trois Frères at the Exhibition costs at least 7/- or 7/6 each; our one room, on the 3rd floor, is £1 a night, and all other charges in proportion. So that Vienna, always, I believe, a dear place, is certainly not now so cheap as it is made out to be.

We came to Linz this afternoon, by train, through very pretty country, which we had meant to see by going up the Danube. We had not time for this, however, as it takes 20 hours or more by the steamer, and it really is not the weather for enjoying excursions by water. We had a beautiful peep of the Danube at the strikingly picturesque village of Melk, the line skirting the waters edge for some time.

CHAPTER XI

Austria and Home

Friday, 30 May. We rose early this morning to have a short stroll before starting by the 8 o'clock train, walked across the bridge over the Danube, which is very picturesque at this point, and took a turn in the large market-place. Then we had an excessively slow journey to Gmunden, doing the 42 miles in 5½ hours! We had to change at Lambach and go from thence by a little single line, which wound about and curved along, through fields and woods, and between tall hedges, like a little country lane. The country is very pretty, and remarkably richly wooded, and seems fertile and prosperous. The women all wear black hoods, completely hiding their hair, and work very hard, dragging carts, and being harnessed to the shafts like a horse, or like a dog, for that is about the most popular draught-animal in this part of the world. The men are handsome fellows, who take life easily, and smoke perpetually.

We had a delicious afternoon at Gmunden. We had meant only to take lunch there, and then go on down the Traunsee to Ischl, but we were so intensely charmed with the loveliness of Gmunden, that we felt it would be a sin to tear ourselves away from it so soon. So we strolled about, through the little town and along the banks of the lake, and then up in the hills, enjoying all the time the most lovely views, for the bright gleamy showery afternoon was just the weather best suited for shewing the varied beauties of this the prettiest lake in the world. The Traunsee reminds one somewhat of Derwent Water, only its banks are more richly wooded, and the mountains that cluster round it are from 5000 to 6000 ft. high. A long chestnut avenue 1½ miles long, stretches along the shore of the lake in front of the houses. We are in a comfortable Hotel, looking out full upon this splendid view.

Saturday, 31 May.   A dull rainy misty English-lakesy morning. We had fixed to start on our drive to Ischl at 8.30 a.m. and rose early in prospect, but the weather looked so unpromising that we waited on and on, gazing anxiously at the clouds, and consulting the landlord as to the state of a benighted little used-up barometer he had. At last at 10.30, we despairingly set off, in a little open carriage, on our 24 miles drive, and it only rained a very little, in a paltry undecided sort of way, though the mist never completely lifted itself from the mountains. Still we enjoyed the drive, which even under such circumstances, was extremely fine, but when we reached the large and handsome Hotel zur Kaiserin Elizabeth, at Ischl, it became clear that we were in for a regular soaking wet afternoon, and there was nothing for it but to make ourselves comfortable indoors. Happily this most civilized hotel is well supplied with Times and Illustrated and no end of Tauchnitz novels.

Sunday, 1 June.   Rain! rain! rain! heavy, persistent, unceasing. There is an English church service in the Hotel, so we went in to it, solemnly putting on our outdoor garments, though it was the very next room to our room. There are about 30 English people in the house, and they look very nice, but we haven't made friends with any of them. It is as cold as Christmas, and after church everybody clustered together round the readingroom fire, clad in comforters and sealskins, velvets and rugs, shivering, and anathematizing the weather with chattering teeth. At 3.30 we could stand it no longer, so we took a closed carriage, and drove back to Gmunden, deciding that it was better to begin the homeward journey a day earlier than we had intended, and so have a day to spare for Aix la Chapelle, rather than lingering on hopelessly in the rain-visited Salzkammergut. So we took the train at Gmunden, and made acquaintance on the way from there to Wels with a regular fire-eater, an Austrian officer, magnificent in uniform, gigantic in stature, Austrian in appearance, but really a countryman of our own. We had a good deal of talk with him, for he waited with us at Wels more than an hour for our train, though his carriage was standing ready at the door. He has been in the Austrian army 30 years, fought in the Turkish Contingent in the Crimean war, and now is Colonel of the Garrison at Wels. And very very dull he must find it, for he told us that his chief amusement was to take the train down to Gmunden, and sit at the Station watching the arrivals and departures. He seemed to regard us as a perfect God-send in his life of ennui. He told us he was a firm friend, but a fierce unrelenting enemy, and we could well believe it. The officers have it all their own way in Austria; this man was travelling without a ticket, cooly 'supposed he had forgotten it' and the guard ventured no remonstrance.

Monday, 2 June. As we are now travelling straight on, disregarding days and seasons, it fell to our lot today to make our journey on Whit Monday, greatly to the diminution of our comfort, as will shortly appear. We had been travelling all night, from Wels onwards, very comfortable, in one of these delicious Austrian Coupés. At 7.30 we reached Nuremberg, where we had half an hour's wait, to be employed in toiletting, breakfasting, and surveying the multitudes for the station was absolutely crowded by a vast assemblage of Whit Monday-ites, well-behaved, well-dressed, and well to do. Absorbed in watching these happy-looking people, we all but lost our train, for we suddenly became aware that it was moving away from the platform. It would have been too ignominious to see it go off without us before our very eyes, so we made a dash at it, the friendly guard, who was just shutting our carriage door, preparatory to springing into his van, saw us, and instead of scolding us and then coolly leaving us to our fate, as an English official would have done, he held the door open, running along by it at imminent peril to his own life, helped us on to the step, and then we scrambled into the carriage, for the train was by this time going quite fast. And the sweet man never rebuked us, though it was clearly our own fault, but smiled amicably, and made a jocund allusion to our narrow escape next time he came to look at the tickets. We pursued our way in peace, past many pretty little German towns, of quaint medieval architecture, borrowed so largely by way of model, by Norman Shaw, through Aschaffenburg and Darmstadt, falling in at the buffet at the latter little station with the John Rhodes party, who have been enjoying a few days at Ratisbon and Nuremberg, and have enjoyed it immensely, having had no rain and are now generally triumphant over us and our Salzkammergut experience.

At Mainz we had to change carriages, contrary to our expectations, as we were told that the *only* change, between Vienna and Calais, took place at Köln. From Mainz to Köln we went down the Rhine, I seeing it for the first time, and feeling, truth to tell, very mildly impressed by it. No doubt it is very pretty in autumn, when the vines are all in full verdure, but just now the hill sides are bare and grey, there are no trees, and these we miss dreadfully on coming from a country so luxuriantly wooded as Austria; the little Rhine-towns are pretty and the *real* castles very picturesque, but the sham ruins are simply disgusting. One ought not to see the Rhine early in June, coming down it, and especially after a tour, and such a tour! Above all, a tour which has included *the Danube*. Here, at these numerous little Rhine stations, we began to rue our folly in travelling on Whit-Monday. The crowds at every station were something tremendous, and they soon began filling up the first class carriages. A very respectable party, two gentlemen and a lady, 2nd class, were ushered in, and we received them with politeness. Two third class women, also respectable, followed at the next station, and we bore their advent with meekness, though eight in the carriage was not the acme of bliss on a fearfully hot day. But then a 9th passenger, a third class man, was pushed in by the guard, and several more were on the point of following, when Dearman, roused from sleep by a very heavy man on his toes, suffering from a headache, moreover waxed wrath, blazed out in indignation, told the surly German guard in forcible English, that he had no right to incommode 1st class through travellers by over-filling the carriage with 3rd class local passengers, threatened to get out himself unless the extra passengers were removed, and pushed out first some baggages against the door, viz. my sac de nuit, and his cloak. These the guard seized, and refused to give back, behaving most insolently, though Dearman calmed down at once, and asked him, quite politely, to give back the things. The train moved off, the guard marched away with our possessions, and when at the end of the journey (Köln) we remonstrated with him, he calmly said the things were still lying on the Godesberg platform, and we must telegraph for them if we wanted them. As we could not well wring the wretch's neck, (which would have relieved my mind more than anything else) we saw no alternative, so we meekly sent off a very polite telegram to the Godesberg Station Master, telling him to send the things to Aachen, as we should be stopping there. I predict that we shall never see them again. Happily the things are 'of no value but to the owner' and of no very enormous value to her, but they are just the little everyday things that it is a nuisance to lose in the middle of a journey. Besides the ordinary prosaic but useful 'night things' there are various pairs of gloves, some collars, a few pairs of cuffs, some chocolate, a pair of earrings, a red flannel jacket, a veil, a bottle of oil, ditto of Eau de Cologne, a purse (containing a small mirror, and few score buttons off gloves, two announcements of our marriage, Times and Mercury, and a watch key, but not a trace of money!) some human bones (3000 years old) from the Catacombs of Syracuse, a German dictionary, an eye glass, numerous hairpins, and all my sponges, brushes, and other 'toilet requisites', last, not least, my nice travelling case, containing buttons of all shapes and sizes, needles, cottons, pins, elastic tape, hooks and eyes – in fact all the little et ceteras that go to make the happiness of a woman's life.

We stopped three hours at Köln, dined there, and strolled about the Cathedral, &c., and then went on to Aachen, arriving at 12.15.

Tuesday, 3 June.　　We are stopping at Aachen, instead of going straight on to London, because we have a day to spare owing to shortening our Ischl expedition, and I want to see Katie Benson.[31] We are at the fine old hotel Grand Monarque, of which I had heard much, and with which I am greatly pleased.

This morning we went to Miss Morrath's, saw the good lady, and liked her very much indeed, and then took possession of Katie, who is much grown, and looks very well, and took her to the Cathedral. She had never been inside it before, though she has been here more than a year! The fine old building is being 'restored', and is full of scaffolding, and to judge by the restoration already accomplished, a flaring red

---

[31] Emily's first cousin, aged 12.

and yellow Modern Berlin stained glass East Window, over
which Dearman almost shed tears, the grand old church has a
degraded future before it.

Katie dined with us at the 1.30 *table d'hôte* at our hotel. Oh!
such a grand affair. 250 people dining (Aachen is crowded
with visitors attending a great Musical Festival now going on),
14 courses, and all the food thoroughly well cooked and
luxurious. Then Katie and I had a drive, and in the evening we
went to the final concert of this Festival, and it was a
magnificent one. Our seats, obtained at the very last minute,
were at the very back of all, but in the interval, when
everybody strolled about the pretty Kurhaus Gardens for half
an hour, eating ices and gossiping with their friends, Katie
joined us, and for the second part, Miss Morrath insisted on
my sitting with them, so the six girls made room for me, and I
enjoyed it very much. The singing was all good, Mme
Schumann's playing such as only hers can ever be, and a long
Solo on the Violin perfectly exquisite.

We left Aachen at midnight, after a very pleasant day in the
nice pretty place.

Wednesday 4 June.   Goodbye to the Continent! Hail to old
England, 'perfidious Albion' though she may be called, always
our Mother-land, of which we are triumphantly proud, though
I trust, not insularly blind to her faults and short-comings.
Our very last day of foreign travel dawned as we approached
Brussels at 5 a.m. this morning. We had had but a short and
troubled night, for we left Aachen only at 12.30 (our lost
luggage has, of course, never turned up!) and just having at
last settled in long-sought comfortable positions for the night,
we are unceremoniously turned out. Every man, woman and
child of us, at Verviers. Why doesn't everybody strike?
'Combination' would be a grand thing here! Why does
everybody meekly turn out, muttering anathemas not loud but

deep, venturing no resistance to the handful of officials at whose beck and call we all must come and go? *I*, for my humble part, do attempt a mild resistance. I feign sleep, swathe my prostrate frame in rugs, and remain motionless. A guard comes *'Mademoiselle il faut descendre'*. No answer, heavy breathing. A second guard touches me on the shoulder, *'S'il vous plait, Mademoiselle, il faut descendre'*. *'Je n'ai rien — je n'ai pas de bagages, et je suis bien fatiguée'* murmur I in pathetic sleepiness. Chorus of officials collected round the obstreperous one *'Mais Mademoiselle, vous ne pouvez pas rester, il faut que tout le monde descendre.'* And at last I am obliged ignominiously to retire defeated from the field, to follow my meeker fellow travellers to the *salle d'attente,* feeling all the smaller by reason of the vain resistance I have made, there to be cooped up with 100 other miserable sleepy-looking beings, for nearly an hour, regaining our carriages only at 2.a.m., when everyone is thoroughly roused, and we are to reach Brussels at five! Two hours and a half to 'kick our heels' at the Brussels station, for it is too early for carriages to be out, or we would take a little drive, then to Calais, a very hot journey, and awfully dusty.

Our companions are a young couple returning from their wedding tour (of one fortnight's duration, and spent on the Rhine. How mild it seems to us five months wedded and much travelled beings!) and an old German, with a piping bulfinch.

The usual scrambling lunch at Calais, then a bright fine calm quick passage to Dover, back to English faces, English voices, English railways, swift of speed, and English railway porters in greasy corduroy. Back to England, glad to be back, after a tour of variety, pleasure, beauty and unalloyed success, such as can hardly be surpassed.

914 BI
Birchall, Emily
   Wedding tour

M L✓